── LET'S DRAW ──
BUNNIES

35 Step-by-Step instructional Bunny Drawings

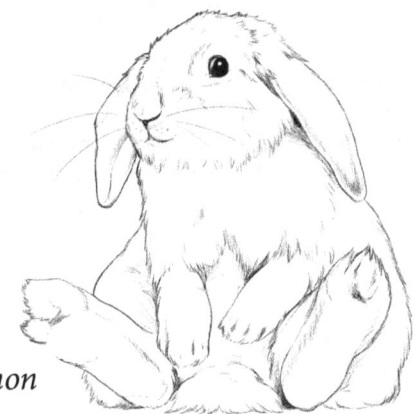

by Lucille Solomon

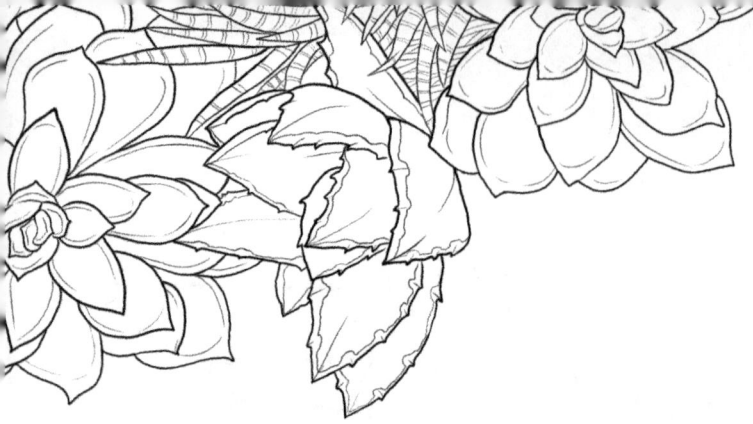
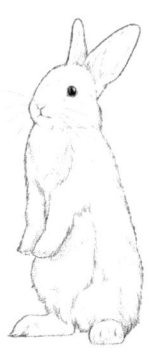

Copyright © 2017 by Lucille Solomon
Illustration Copyright © 2017 by Lucille Solomon

All rights reserved. No part of this publication may be reproduced, distributed, or transmitted in any form or by any means, including photocopying, recording, or other electronic or mechanical methods, without the prior written permission of the publisher, except in the case of brief quotations embodied in critical reviews and certain other noncommercial uses permitted by copyright law.

www.tiny-axolotl.com

First edition 2017

CONTENTS

Introduction	4
Art Tools	5
How to start	6
Drawing fur	7
Drawing a Bunny Head	8

Breeds

English Spot	10
Holland Lop	12
Flemish Giant	14
Rex	16
Deilanar	18
French Lop	20
Lionhead	22
Angora	24
England Lop	26
Netherland Dwarf	28
Wild Hare	30

Step by Step Guides

Singles	32 – 73
Doubles	74 – 81

Coloring pages	82 – 91

INTRODUCTION

The animal kingdom offers a variety of drawing motifs, shapes, and colours. The spectrum of animal species opens up to a seemingly almost endless universe waiting for you to draw.

Why rabbits?

I am the owner of rabbits, and I enjoy their amusing peculiarities and their versatile body language.
I quickly realized that they are a fun, quirky, and of course, a very cute drawing subject.

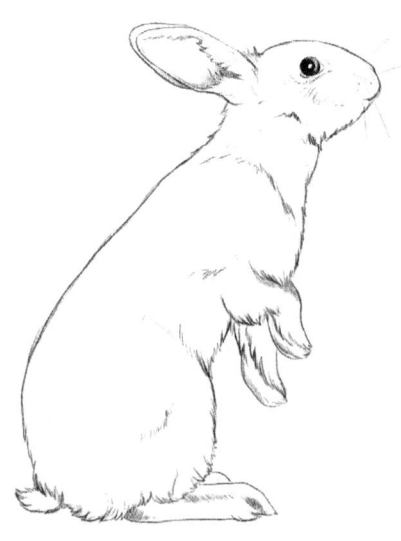

ART TOOLS

If you're just starting out with drawing, pencils would be the most obvious choice. With this simple tool, you'll be able to learn the basic drawing technics the easiest way, and you can also quickly erase little mistakes. Good pencils are marked with either H, HB, or B. These indicate the grade of hardness you're working with.

H leads are extremely smudge-resistant and give cleaner lines, making them useful for outlines, technical drawings, and light sketches. The downside of these leads is that they can be difficult to erase and leave scratches on your paper if you press too hard when drawing.

HB is in the middle of the spectrum and is the standard lead grade used because it's dark enough to appear clear while having minimal smudging.

B leads are smooth to draw with, creating dark, heavy lines that can be smudged but are easy to erase again.

Although it's a matter of taste which grade you choose to work with, I have a particular way of using the different leads:

1. I like to start out with a hard pencil, but I'll only use it very lightly as I try to achieve the general proportions through simple shapes.

2. When these are set, I'll use a kneaded eraser to fade out these lines until they're barely visible.

3. I then go ahead and use an HB lead to add the rabbit's features, the fur, and the details.

4. At the end, I'll use a B pencil to add depth to the eyes and darken the overall drawing.

Of course, you can apply this to mechanical pencils as well and just change out the leads.

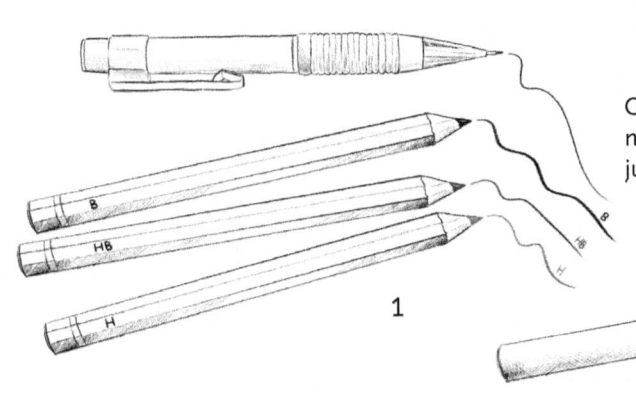

1

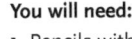

3

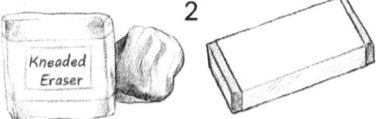

2

You will need:
1. Pencils with different leads: H, HB, and B
2. Kneaded eraser and regular eraser
3. Eraser pencil

HOW TO START

1. The first step is getting the basic proportions right. The easiest way is to start with the head and the body. Usually, we can create the body with one to three circles, depending on the position of the bunny.

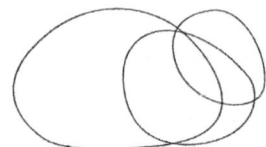

2. For the second step, you'll add the secondary features—the ears, the feet, and a fluffy tail. Amusingly, these shapes usually resemble either carrots or Easter eggs.

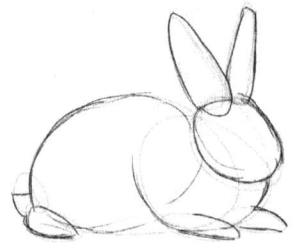

3. In the third step, these lines are faded away with the kneaded eraser. These faded guidelines help you to draw your actual picture. Now you can also add the facial features and details to the feet.

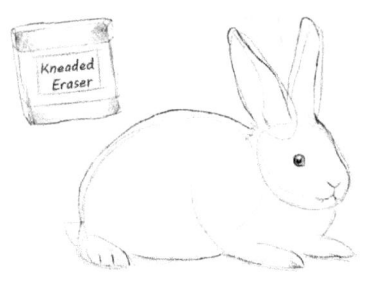

4. This step is my favorite because, now, you can add all the details. By adding shading to the fur, details to eyes—and adding whiskers—the bunny comes to life.

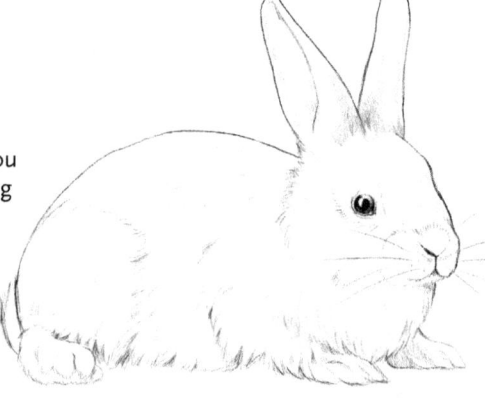

DRAWING FUR

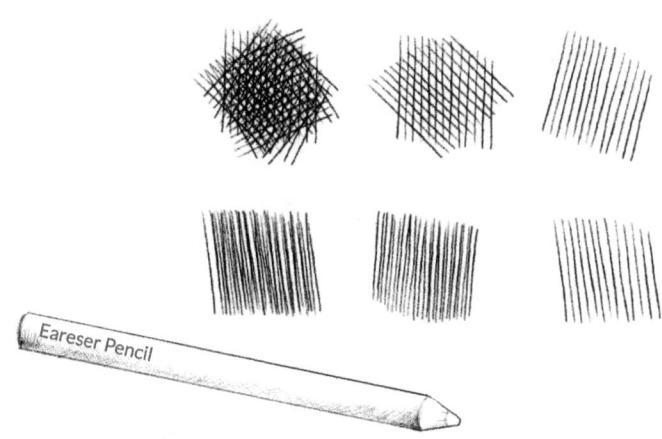

Drawing fur isn't as difficult as you might assume. Follow these easy steps, and you'll be drawing fluffy rabbits in no time:

1. Start off with a few simple sketching exercises. You can build up darkness either through cross-hatching or through drawing lots of lines close to each other.

2. For the second step, you'll be using your eraser pencil. This is a 'pencil' that has an eraser lead instead of a graphite lead. Of course, you can use a regular pencil sharpener to get the sharp point.

3. Now use the eraser pencil to erase a tuft of fur. Depending on the length of fur, you can either draw long streaks or, for short fur, short ones.

4. To give the fur depth, you can use a regular pencil (for some extra darkness, use a B lead) to add shadow and definition under the tuft of fur you just erased.

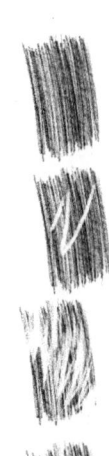

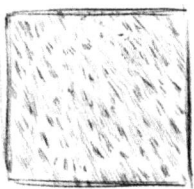 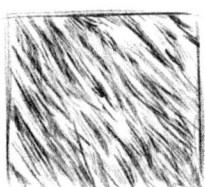 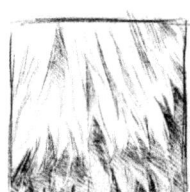 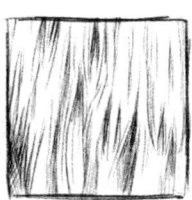

THE BUNNY HEAD

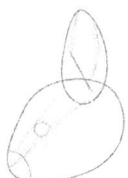 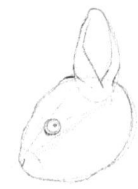 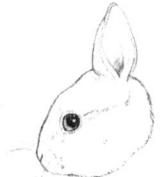

Dwarf Bunny

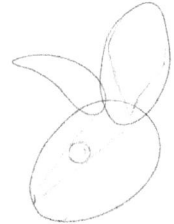 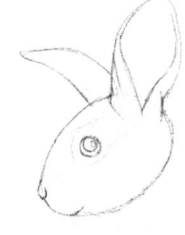 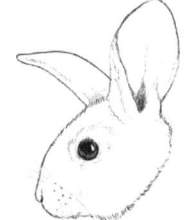

Regular-sized Bunny

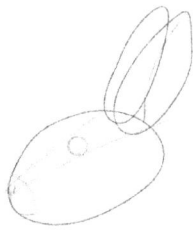 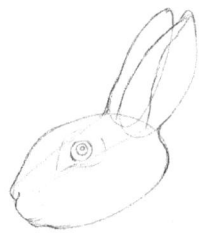 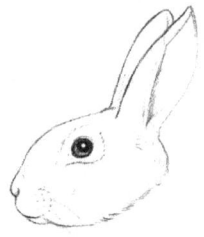

Giant Bunny

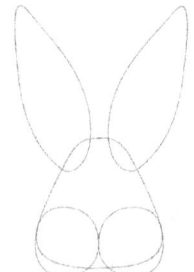 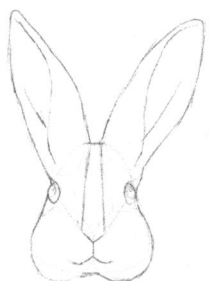 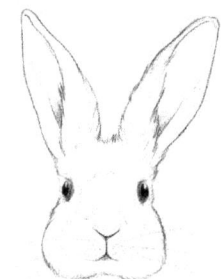

Front View

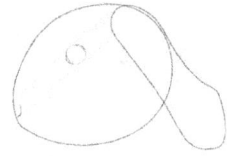 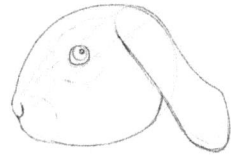 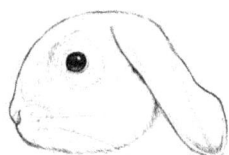

Lop-Eared Bunny

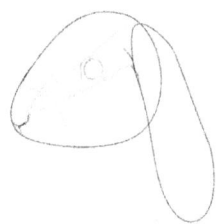 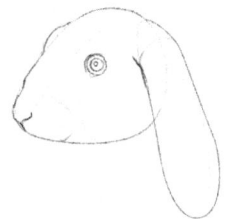 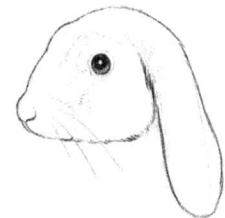

English Lop-Eared Bunny

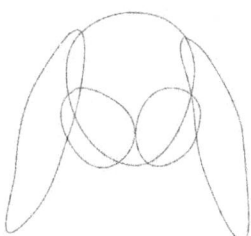 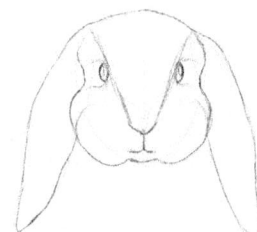 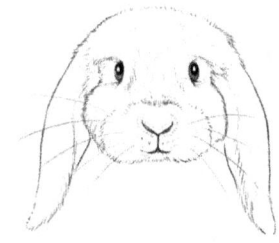

Lop-Eared Bunny
front View

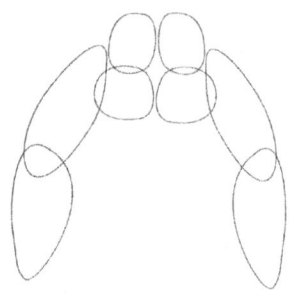 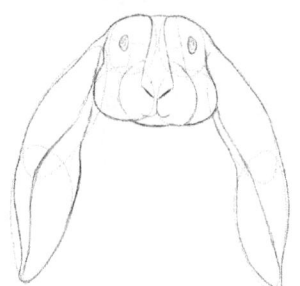 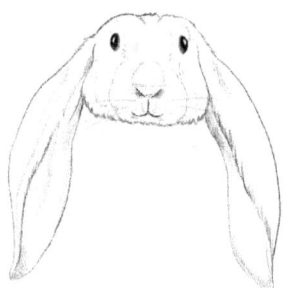

English Lop-Eared Bunny
front View

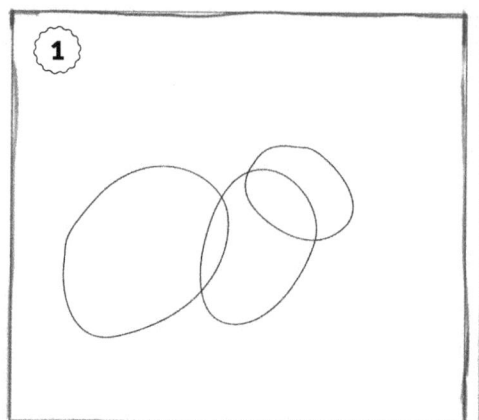
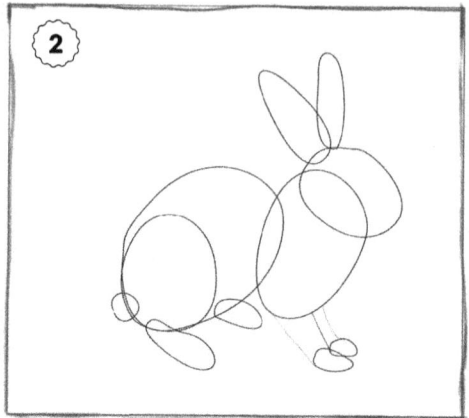

ENGLISH SPOT

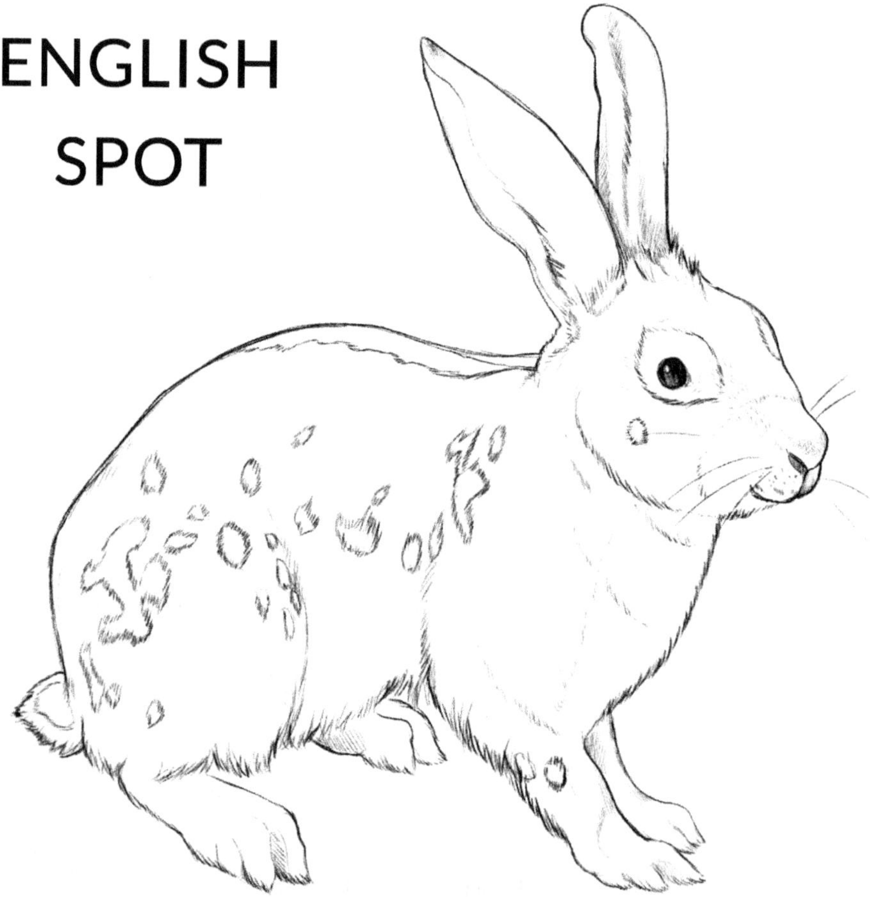

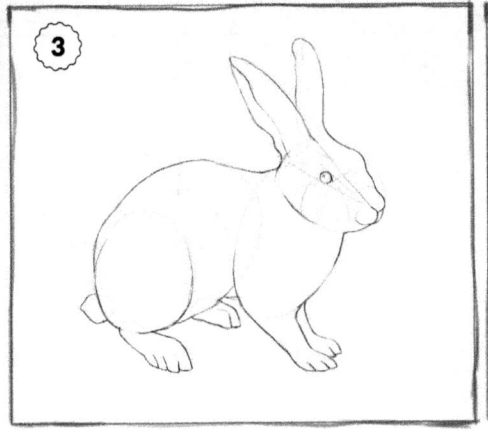
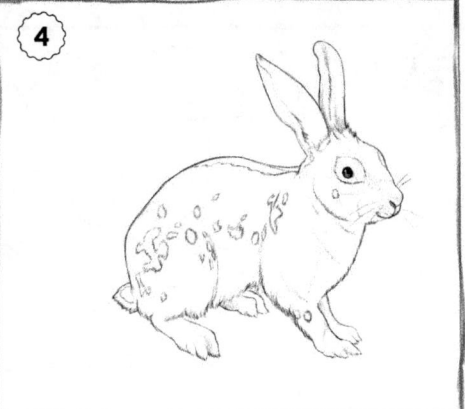

Your turn!

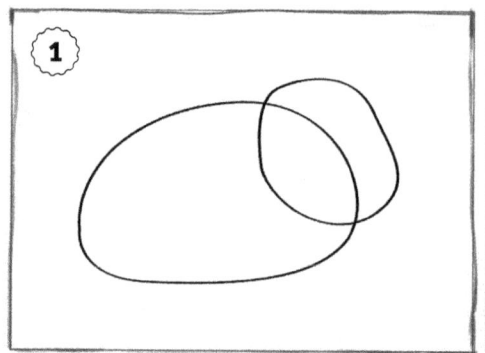
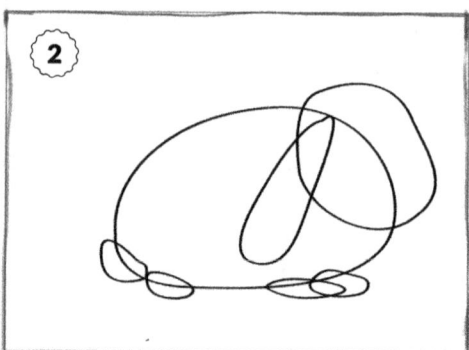

HOLLAND LOP

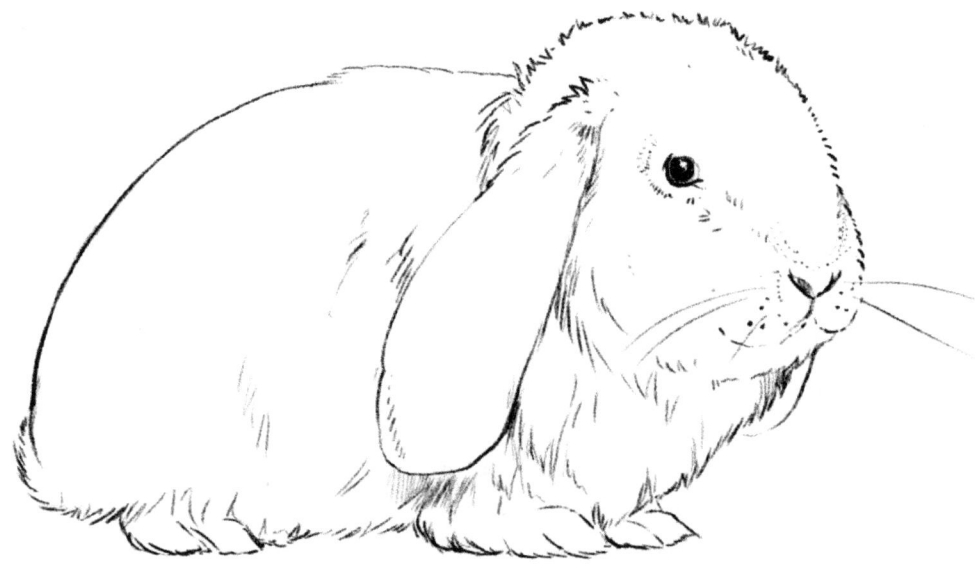

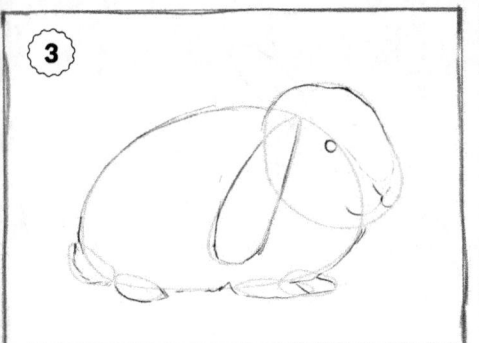
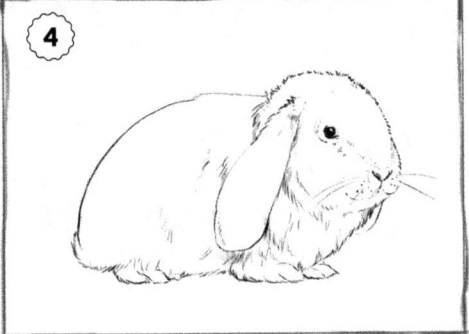

Your turn!

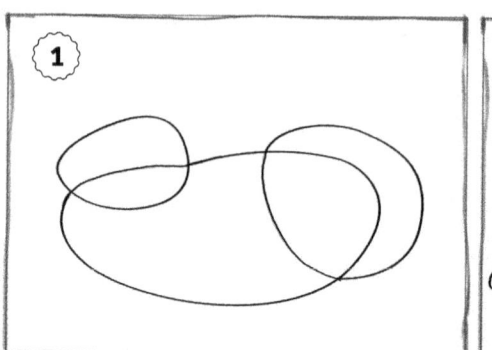
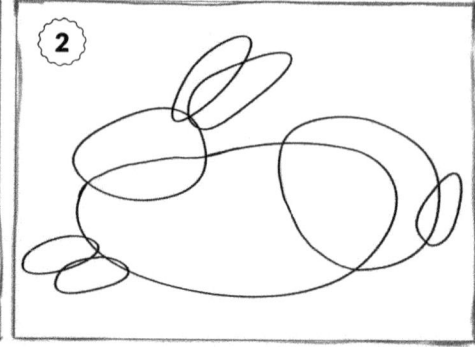

FLEMISH GIANT

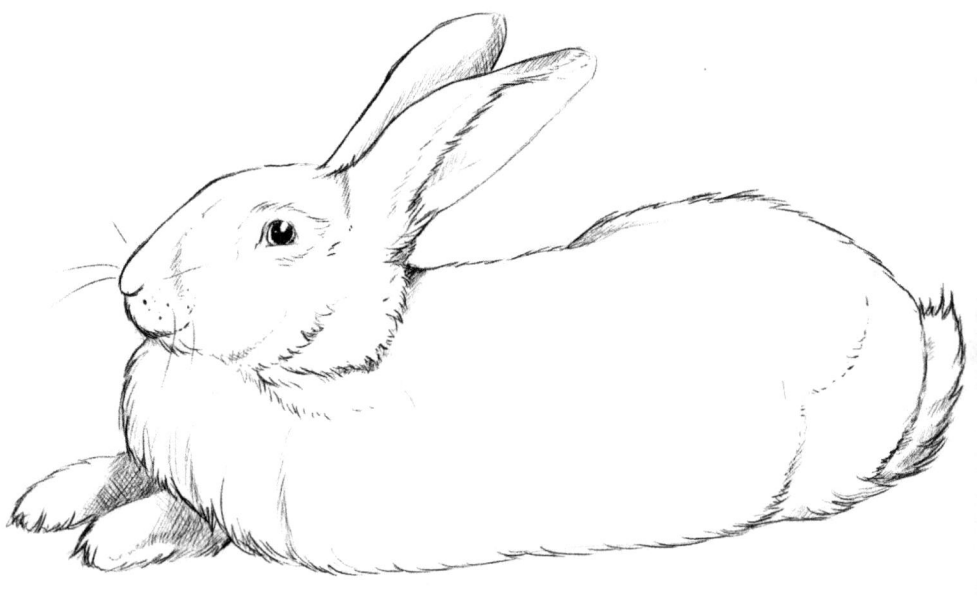

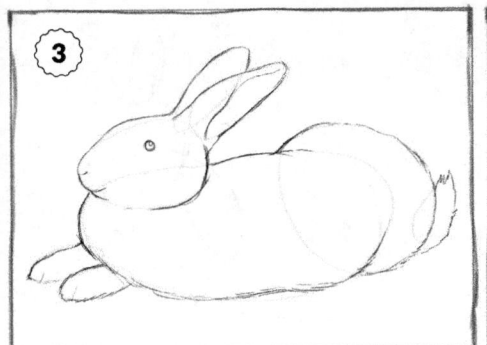
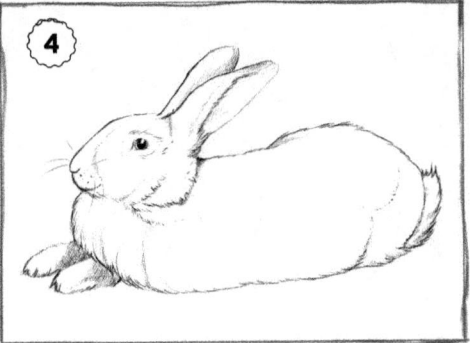

Your turn!

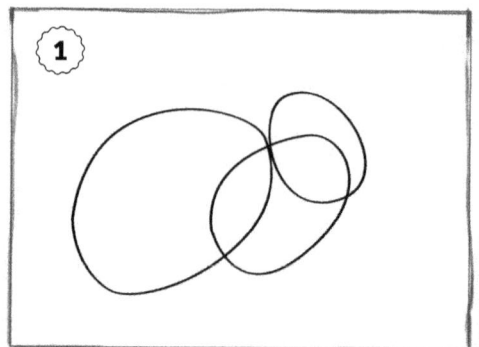 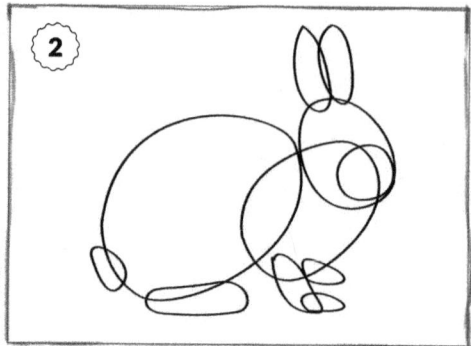

REX BUNNY

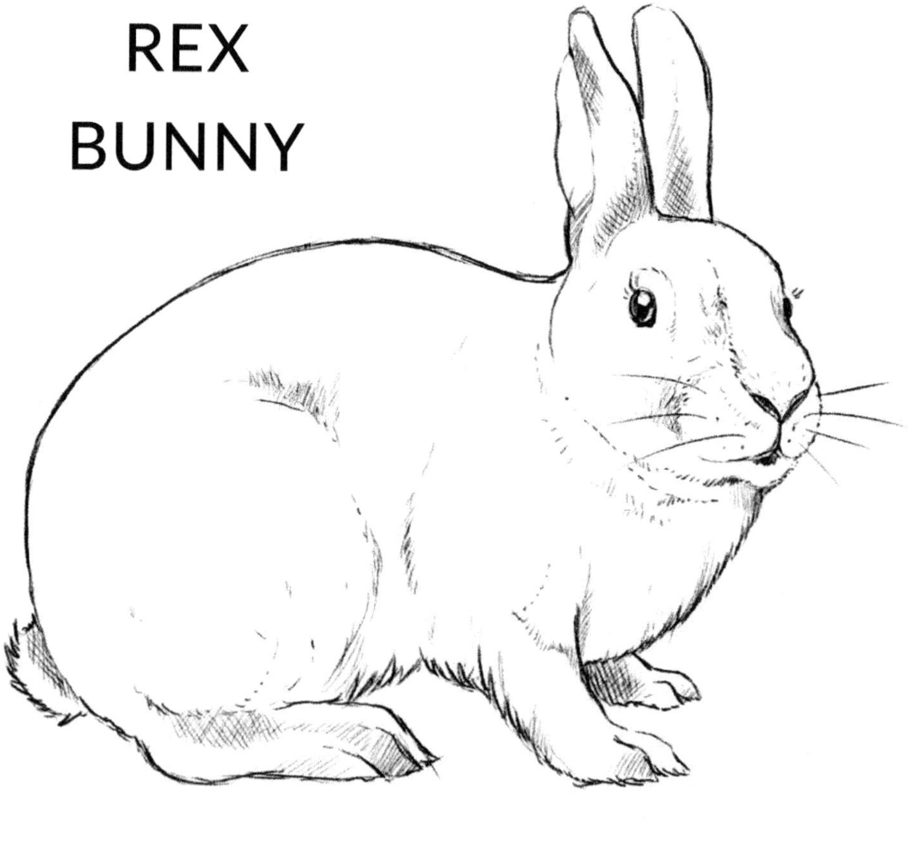

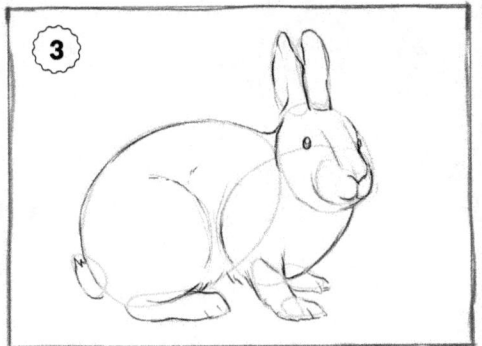
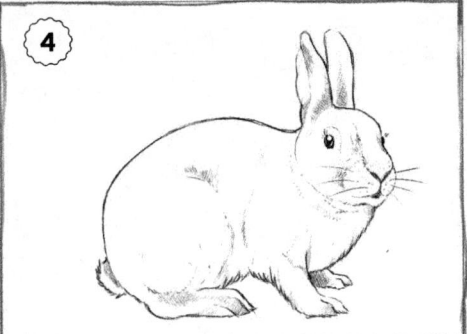

Your turn!

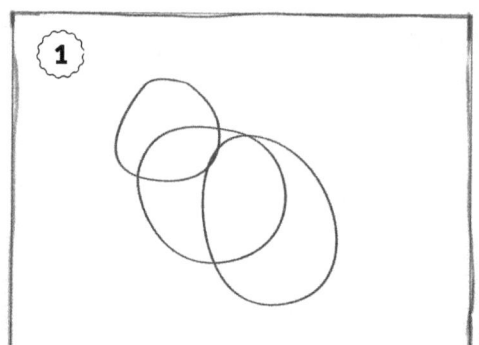
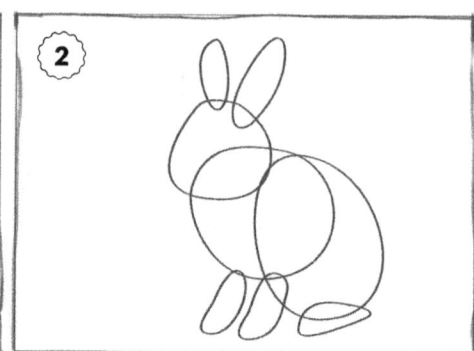

DEILANAR BUNNY

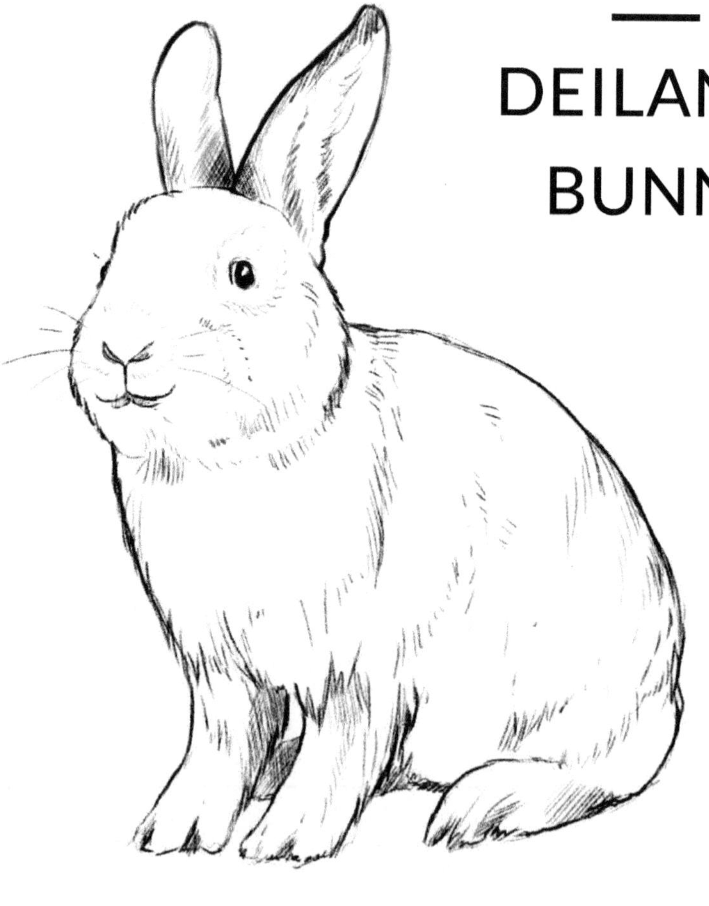

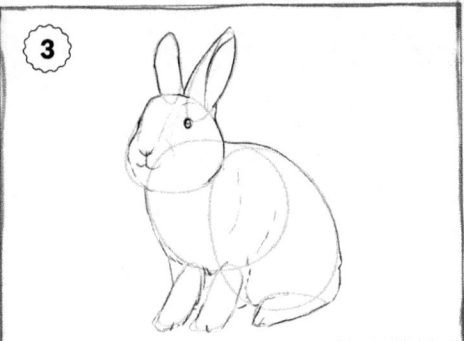
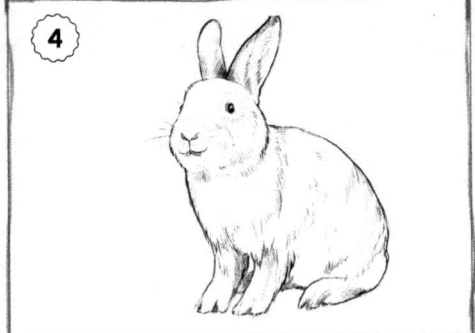

Your turn!

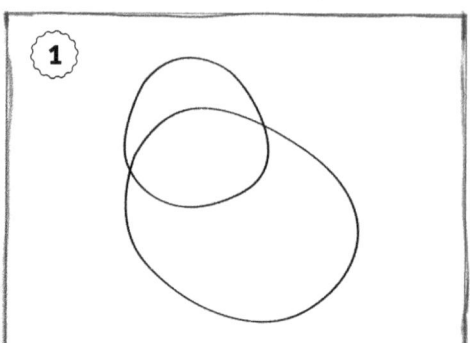
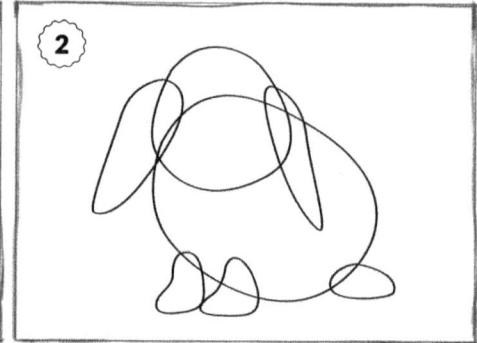

FRENCH LOP

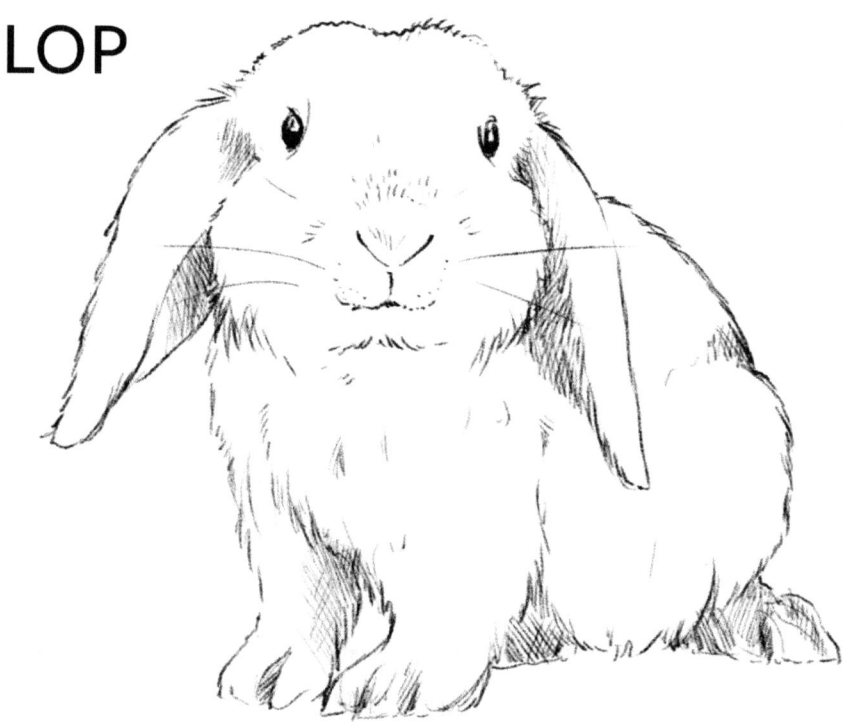

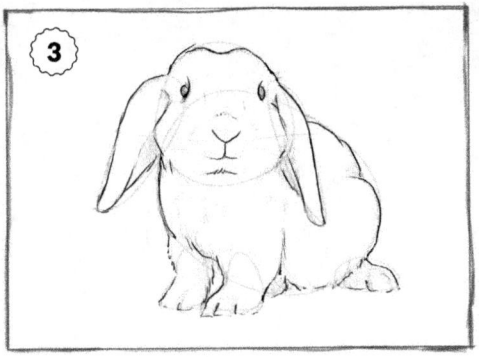
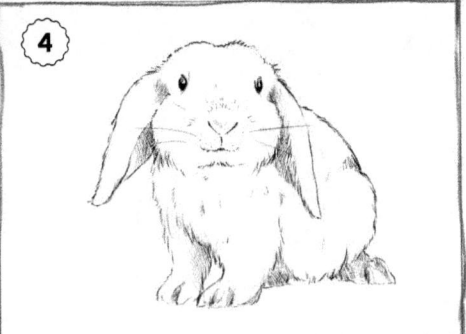

Your turn!

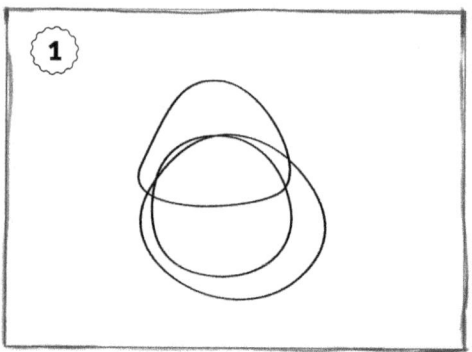
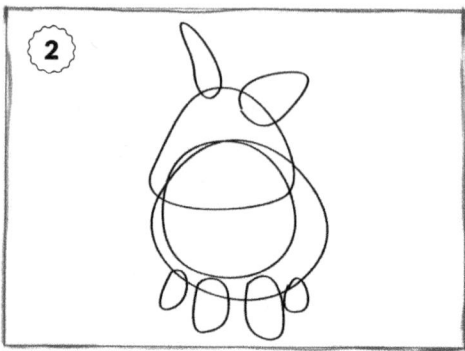

LIONHEAD BUNNY

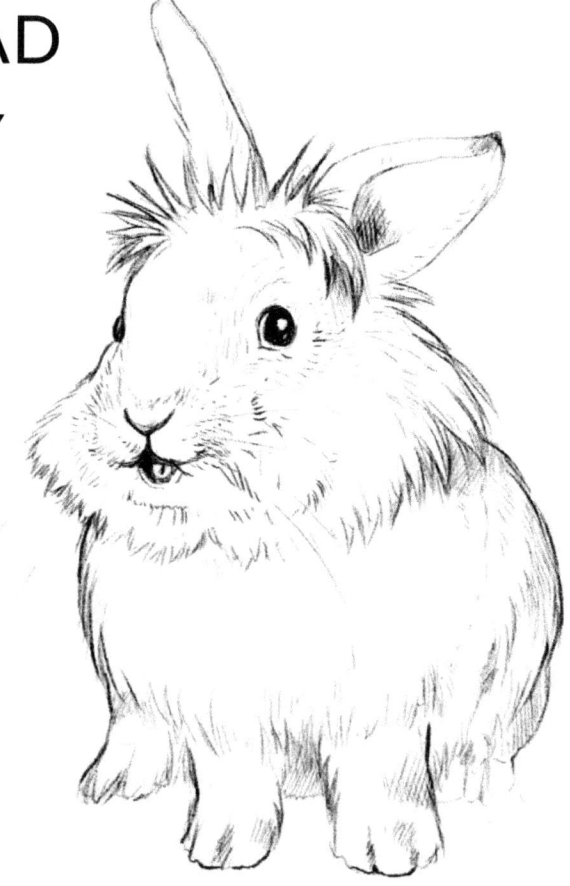

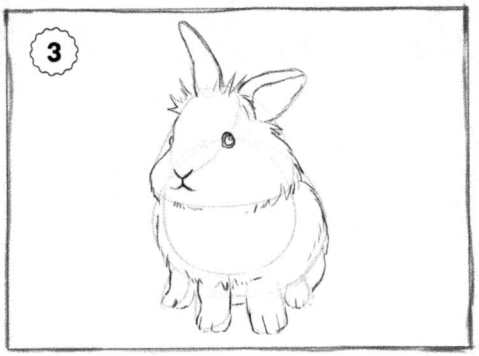
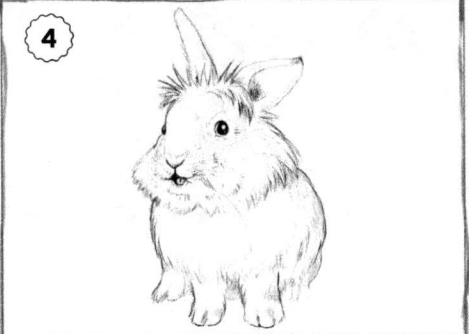

Your turn!

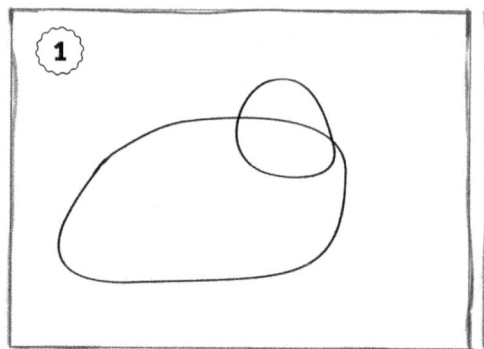
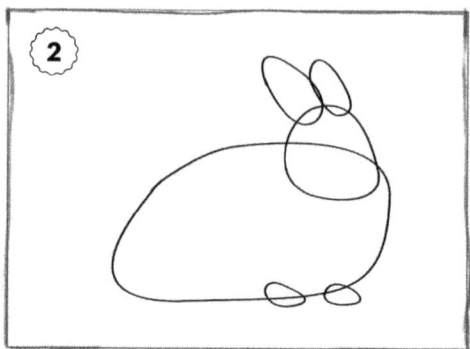

ANGORA BUNNY

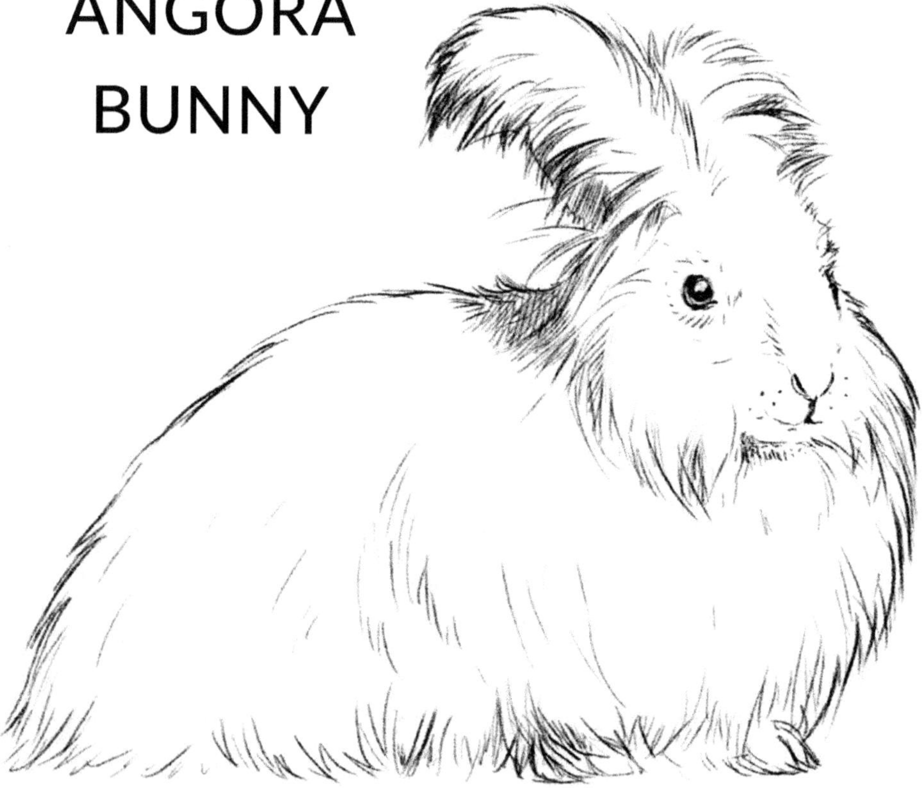

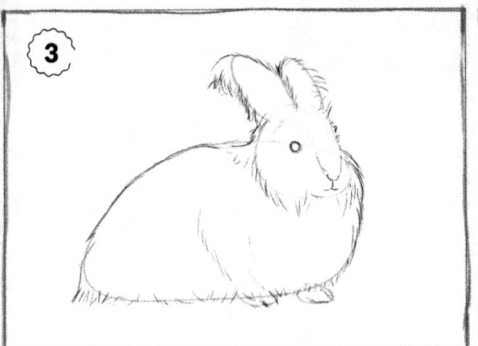
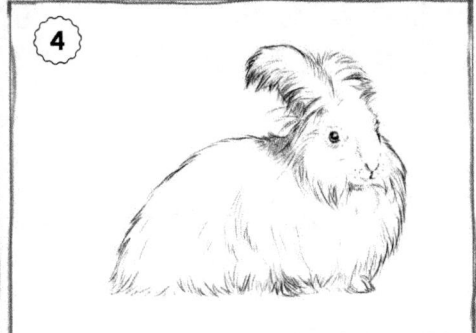

Your turn!

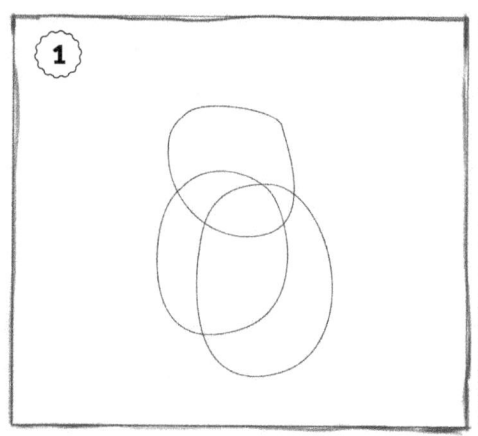
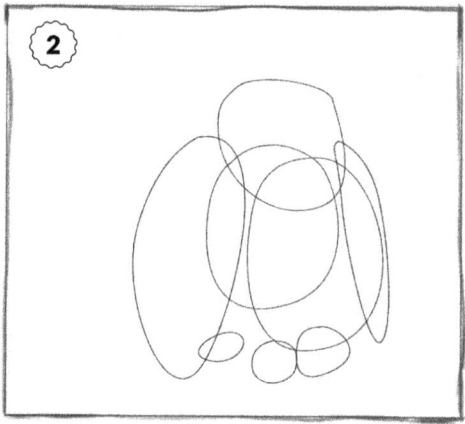

ENGLAND LOP

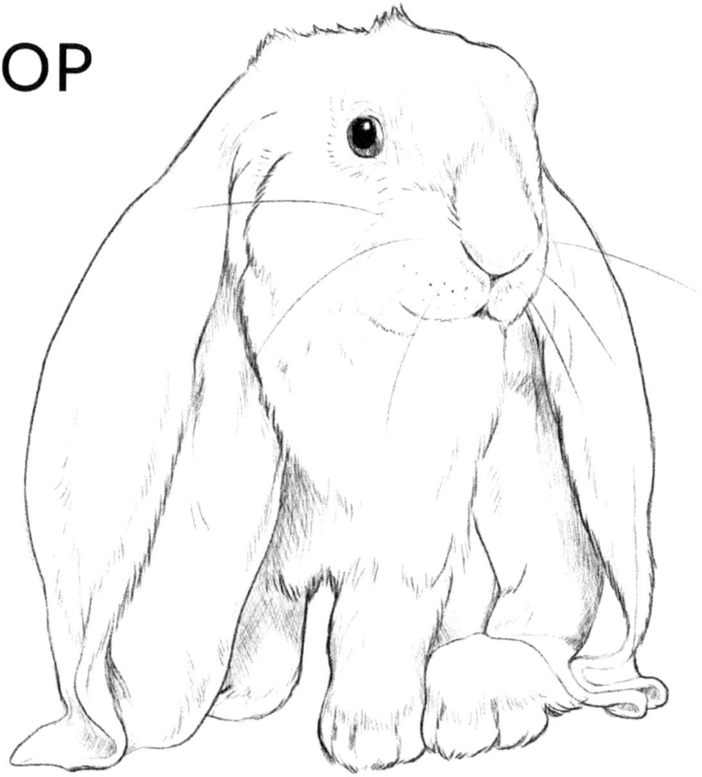

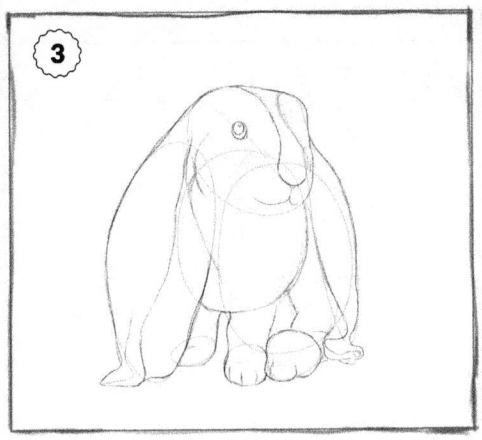
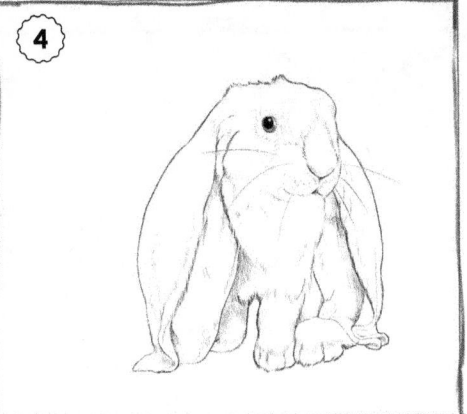

Your turn!

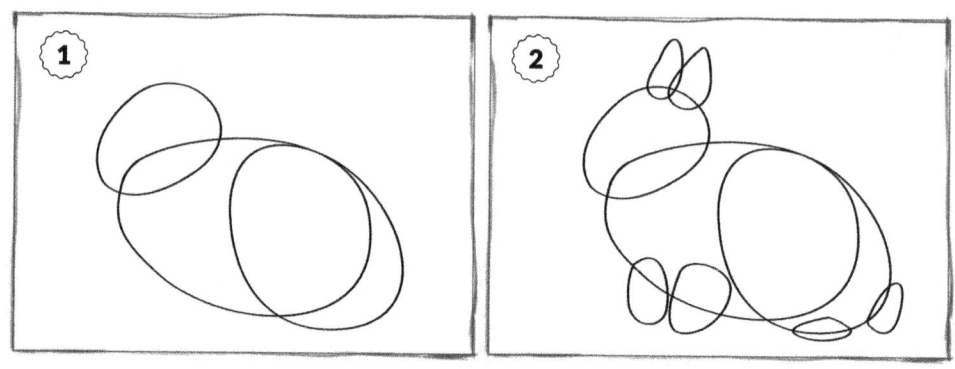

NETHERLAND DWARF

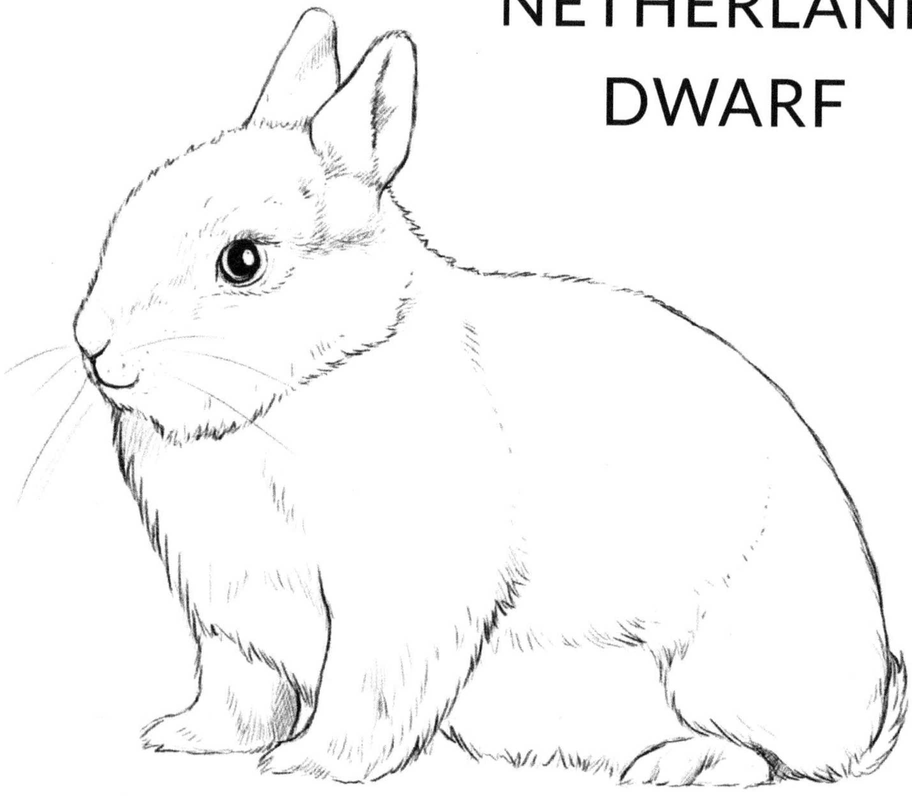

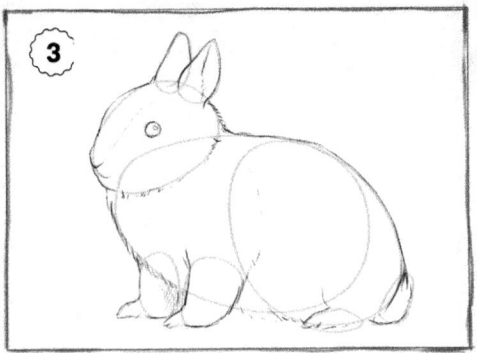
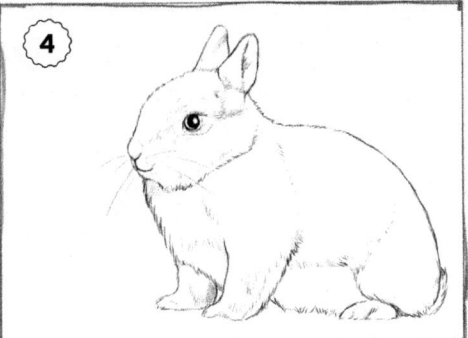

Your turn!

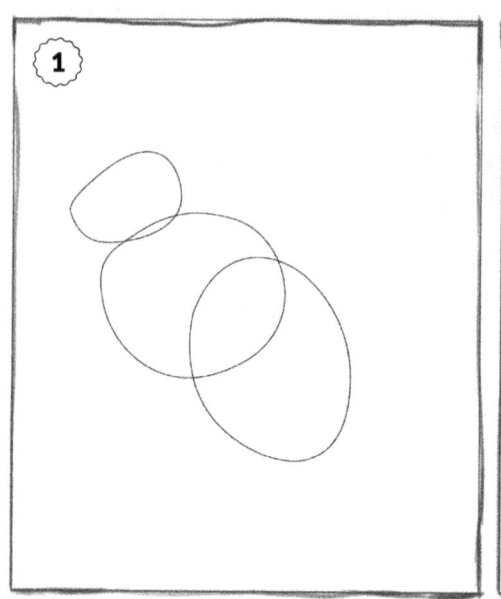
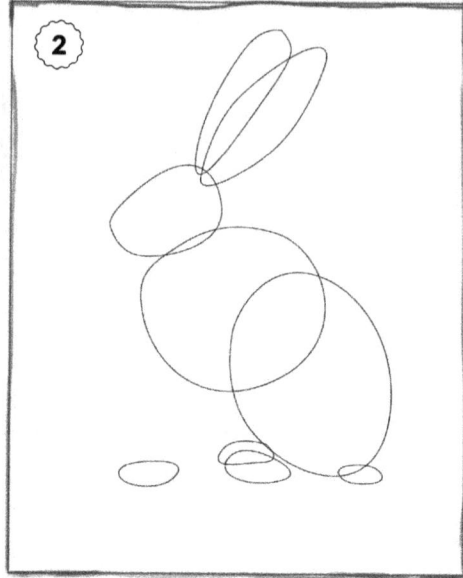

WILD HARE

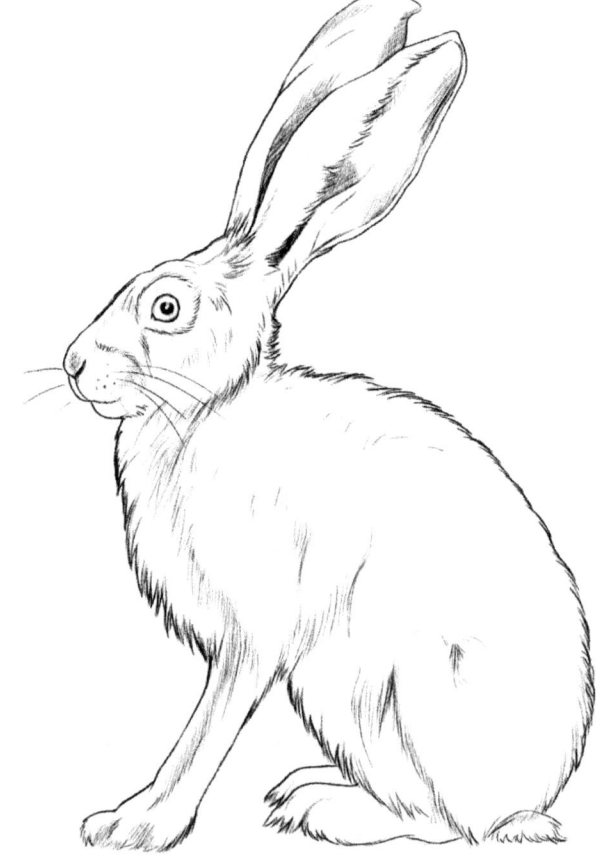

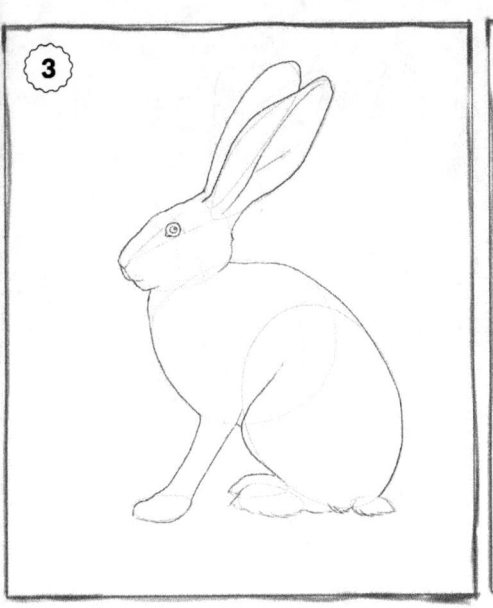
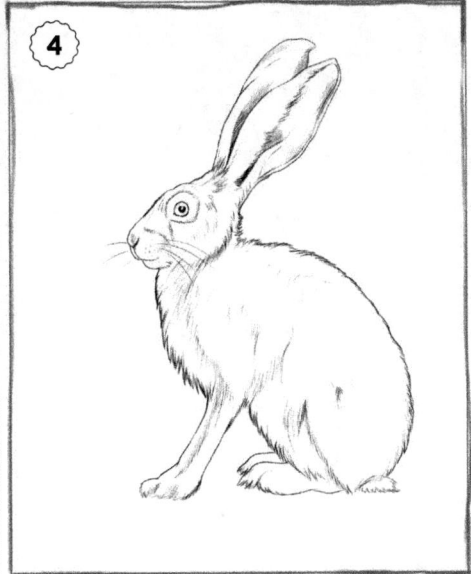

Your turn!

31

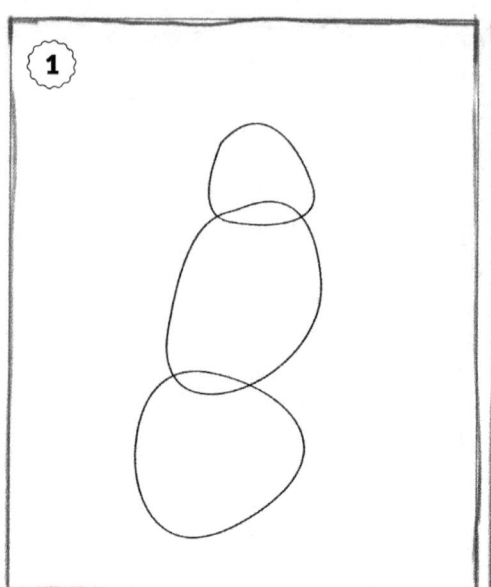
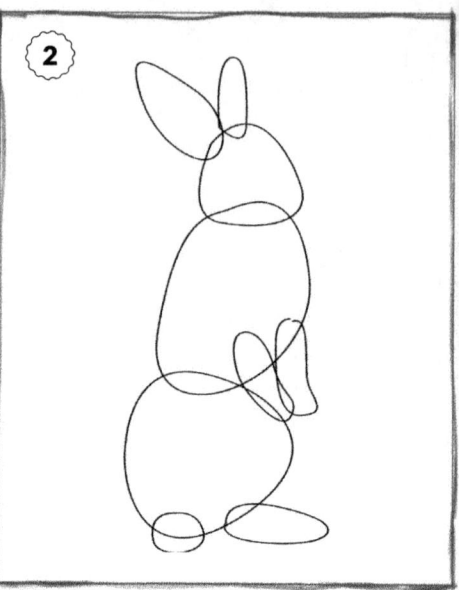
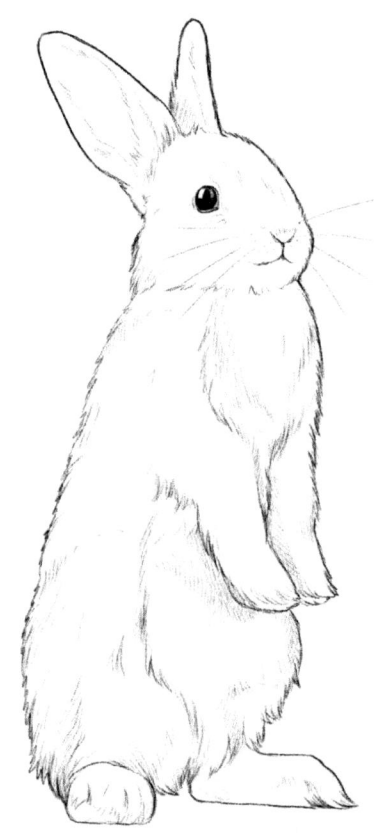

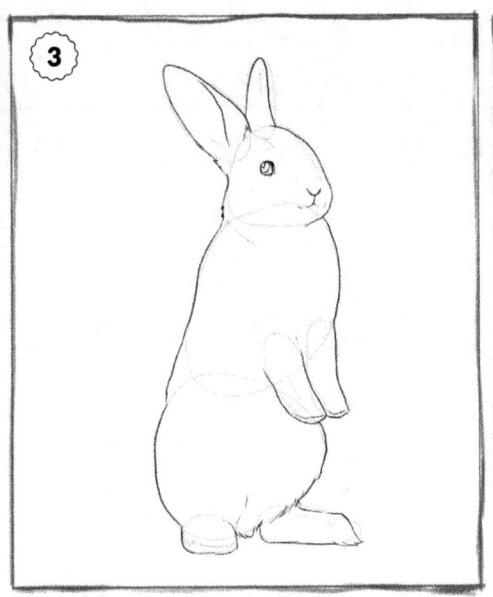
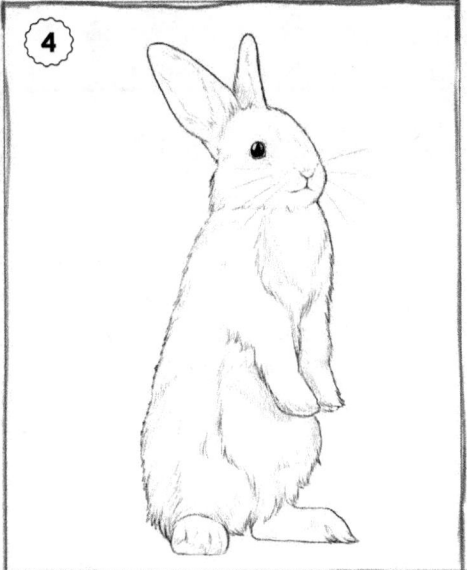

Your turn!

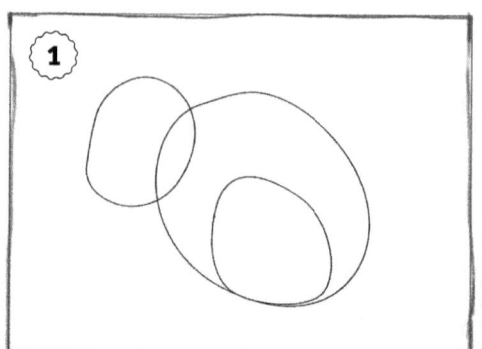
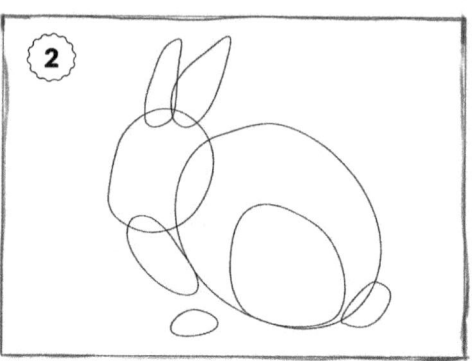
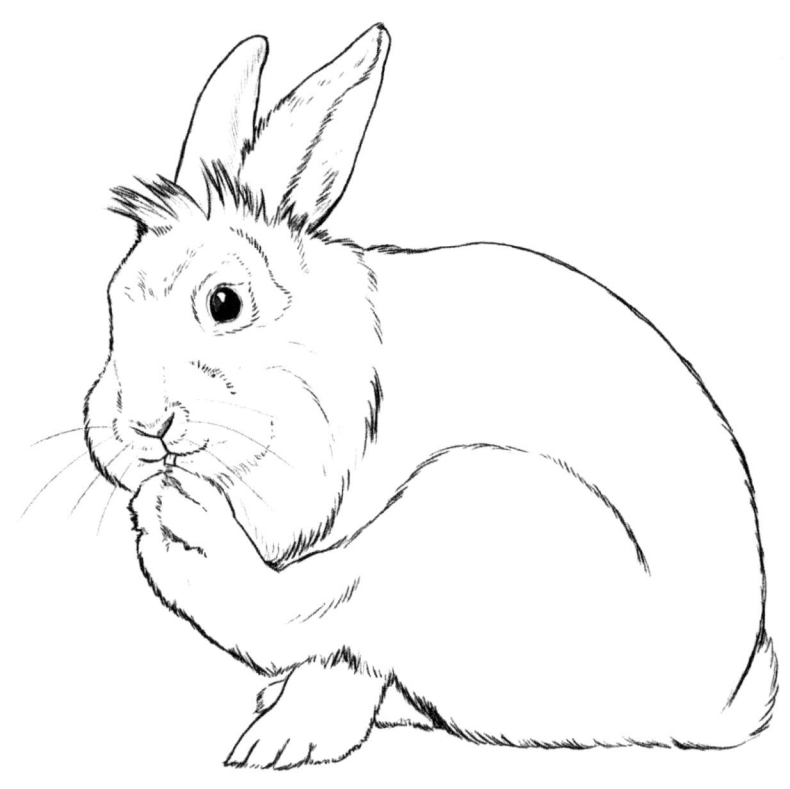

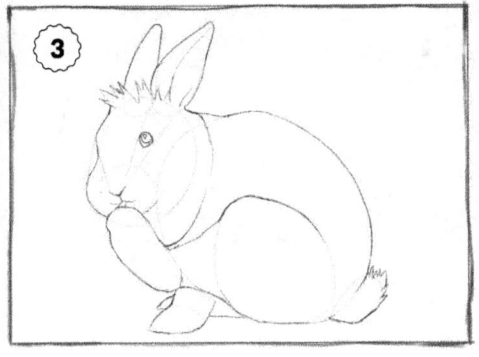
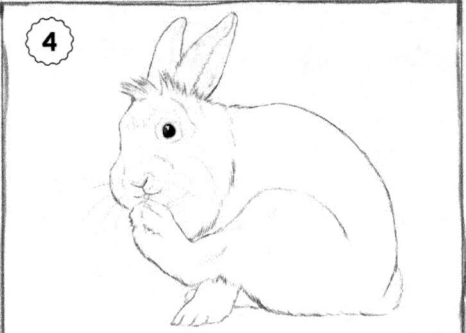

Your turn!

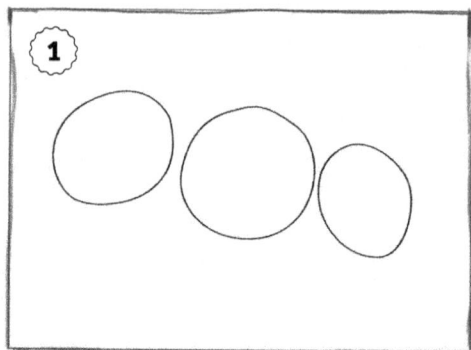
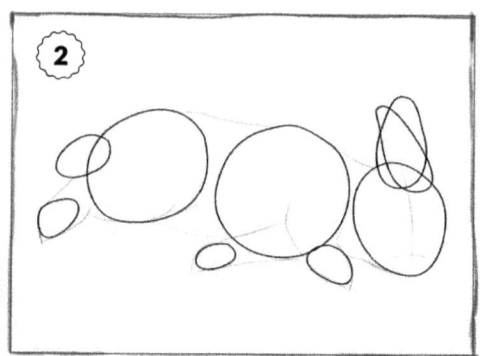
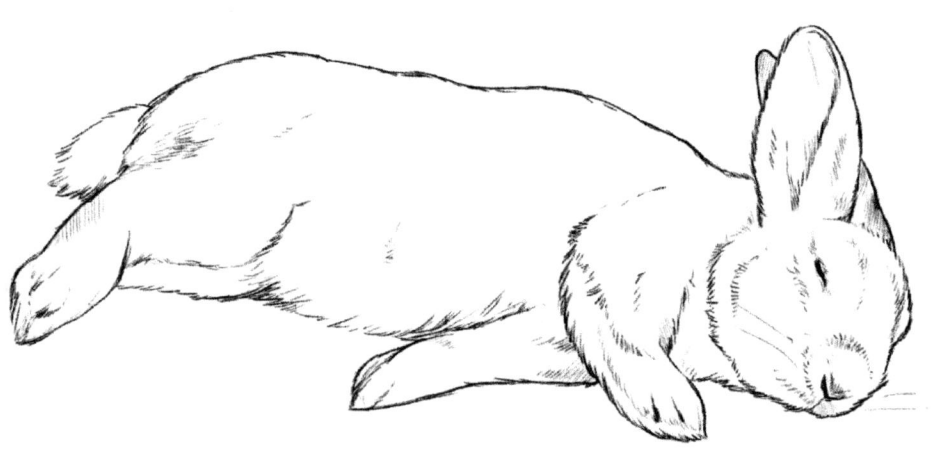

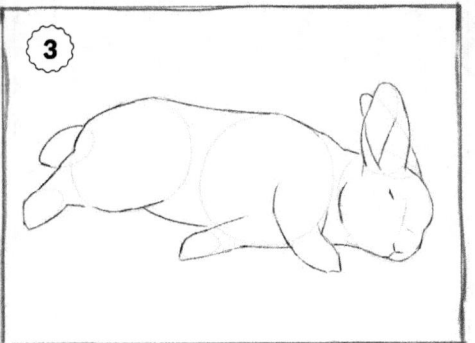
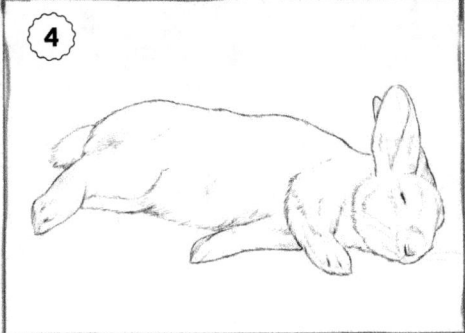

Your turn!

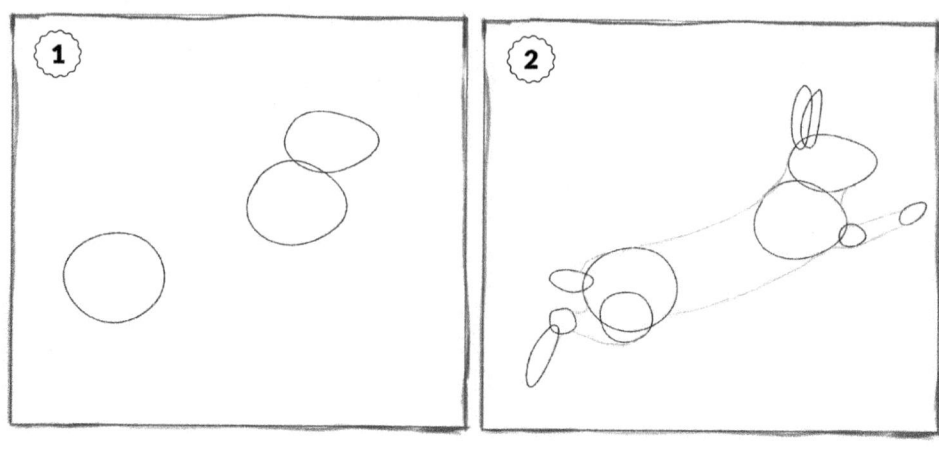
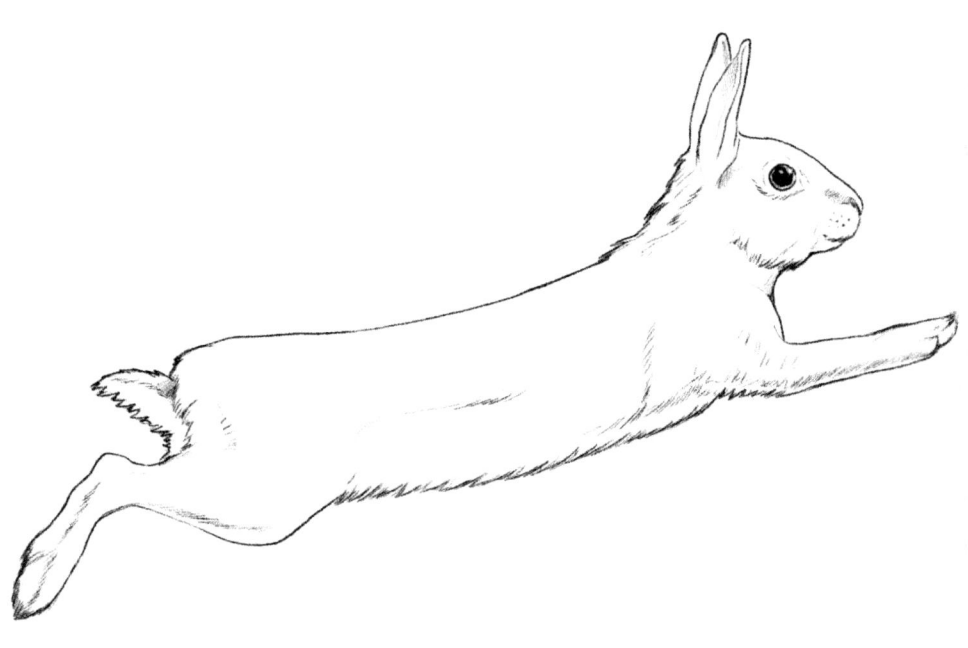

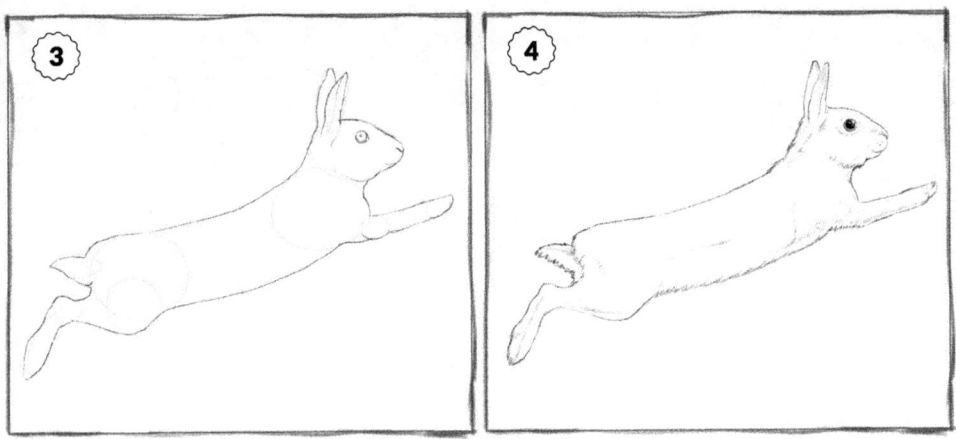

Your turn!

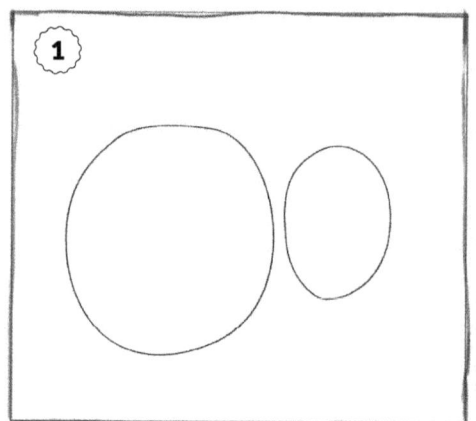
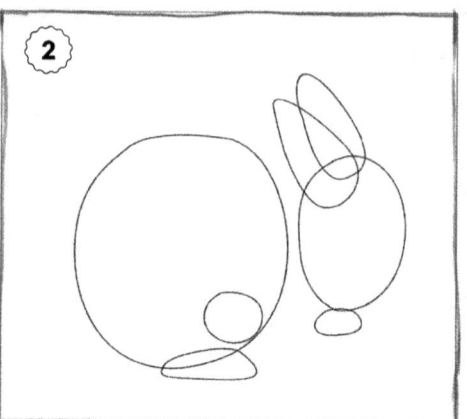

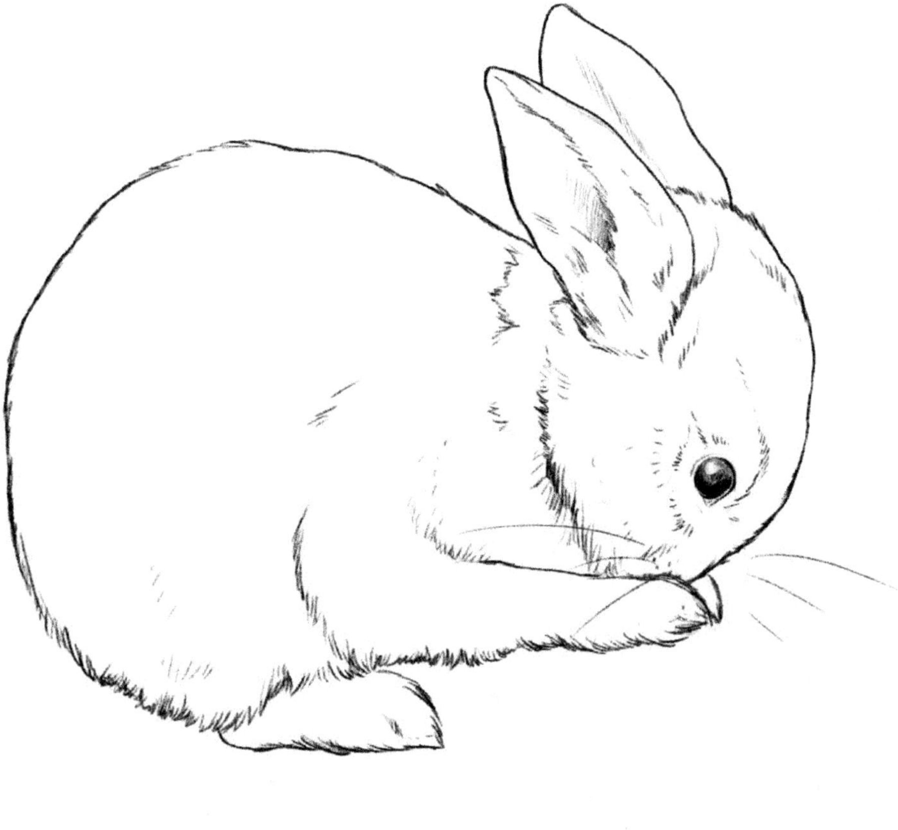

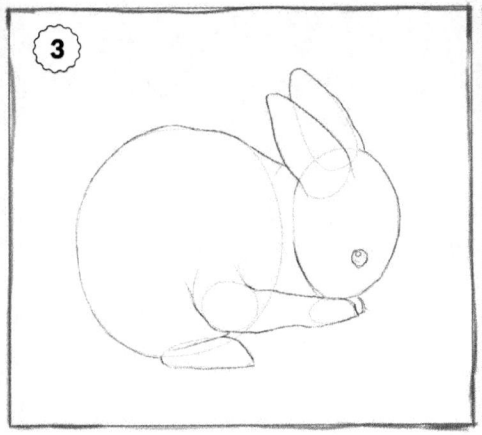
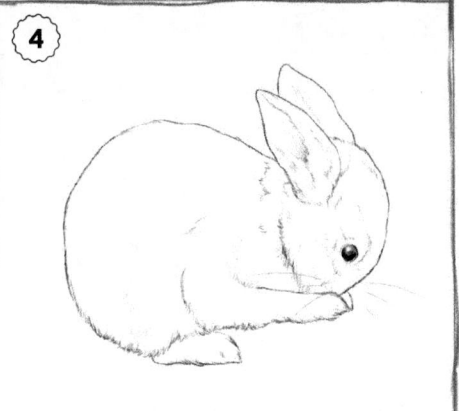

Your turn!

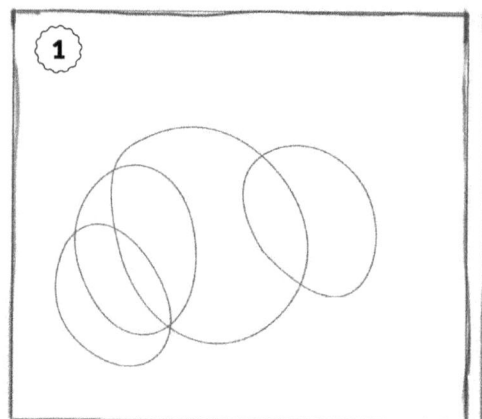
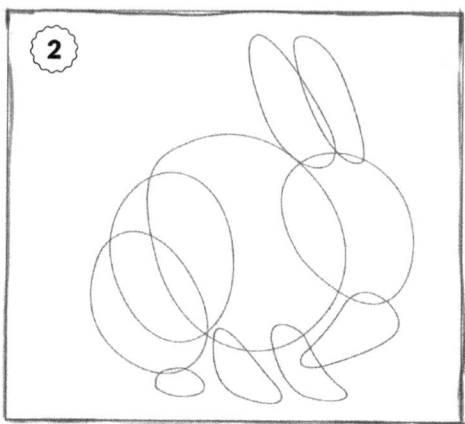
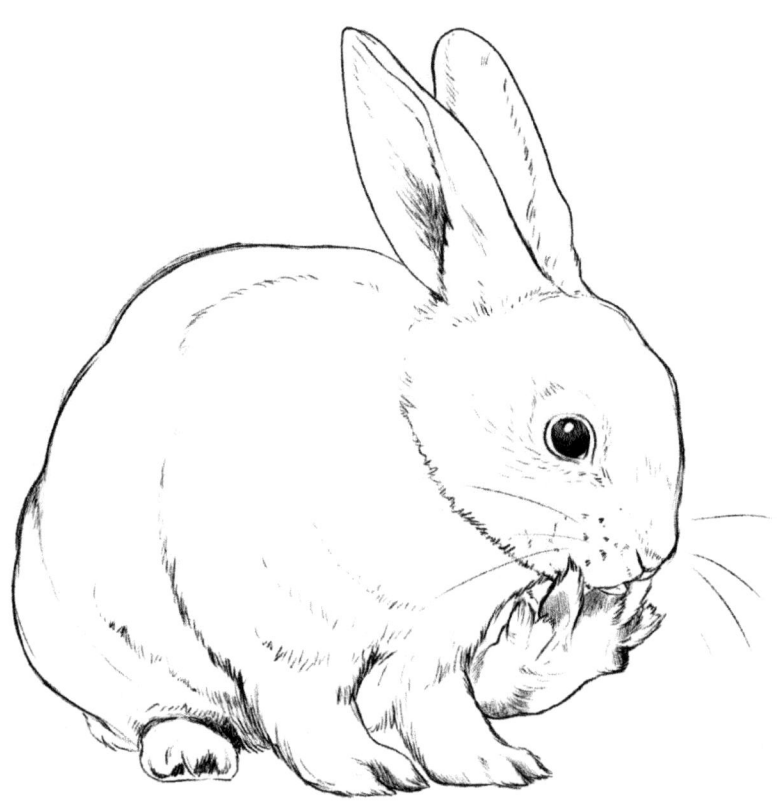

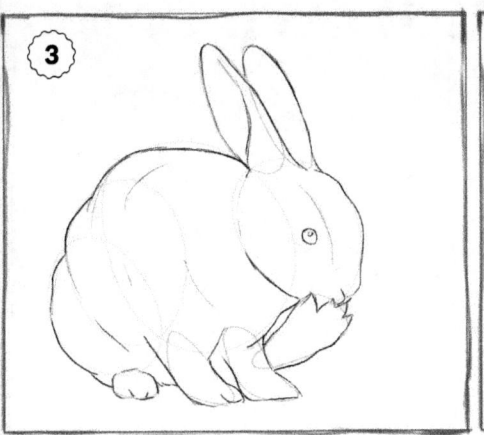
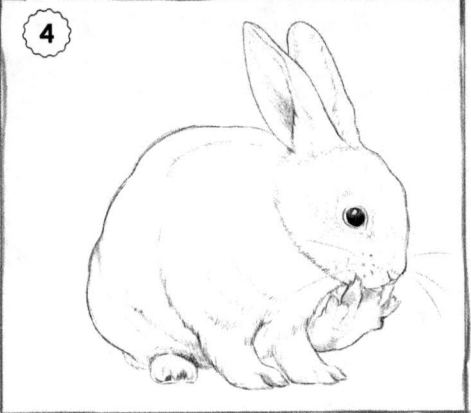

Your turn!

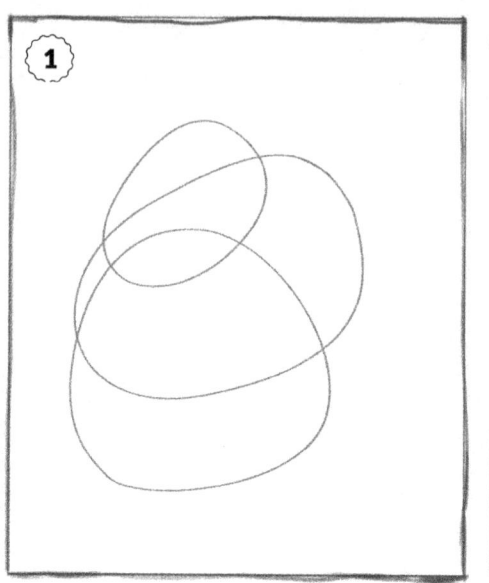
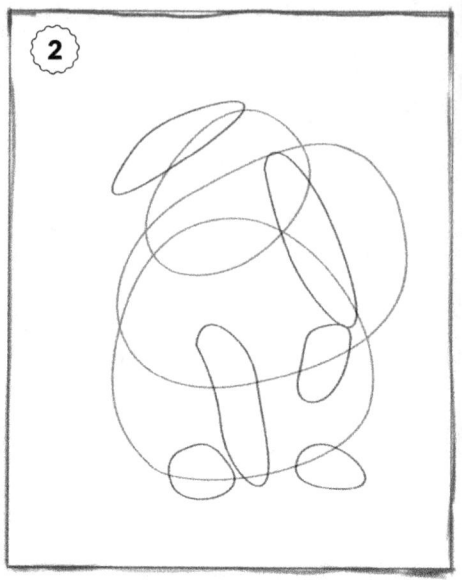
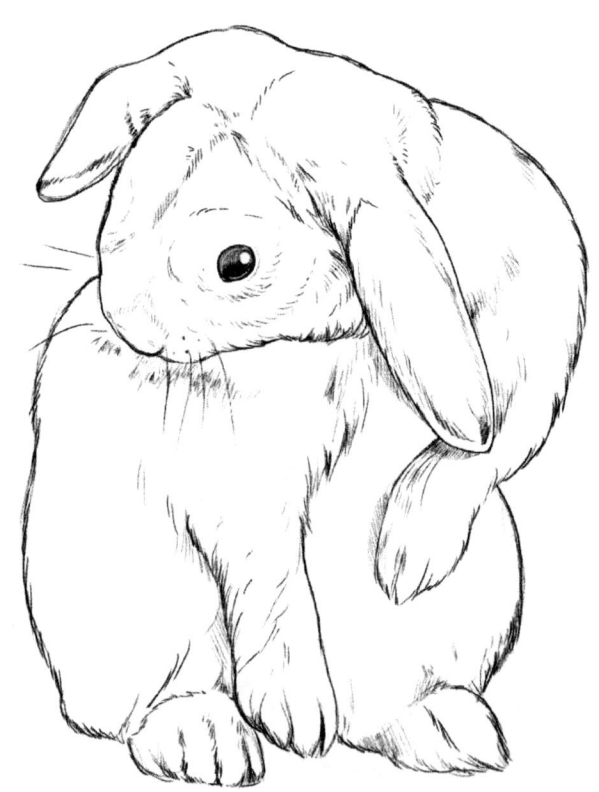

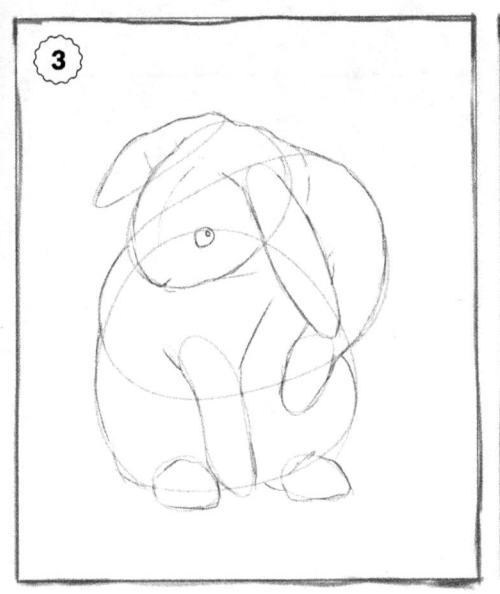
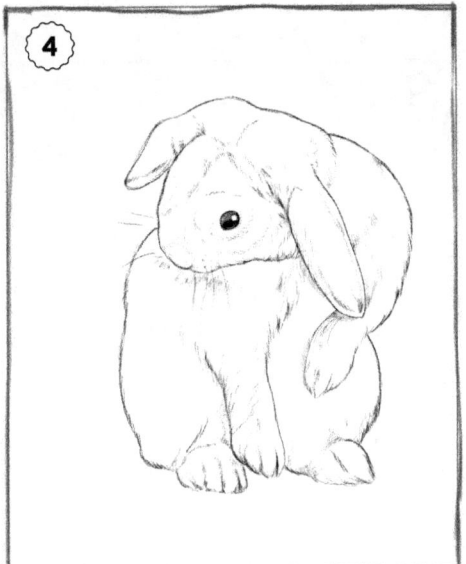

Your turn!

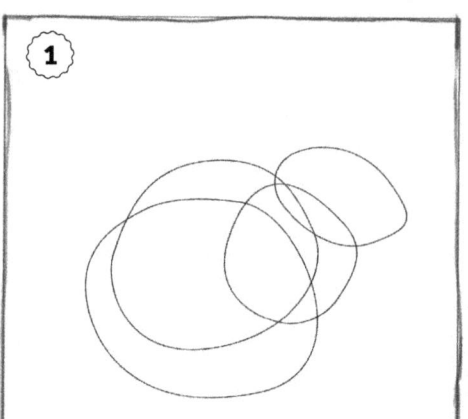
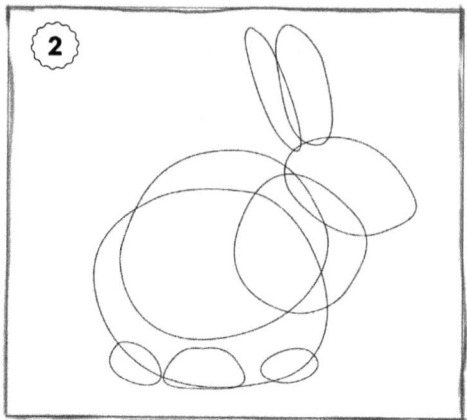

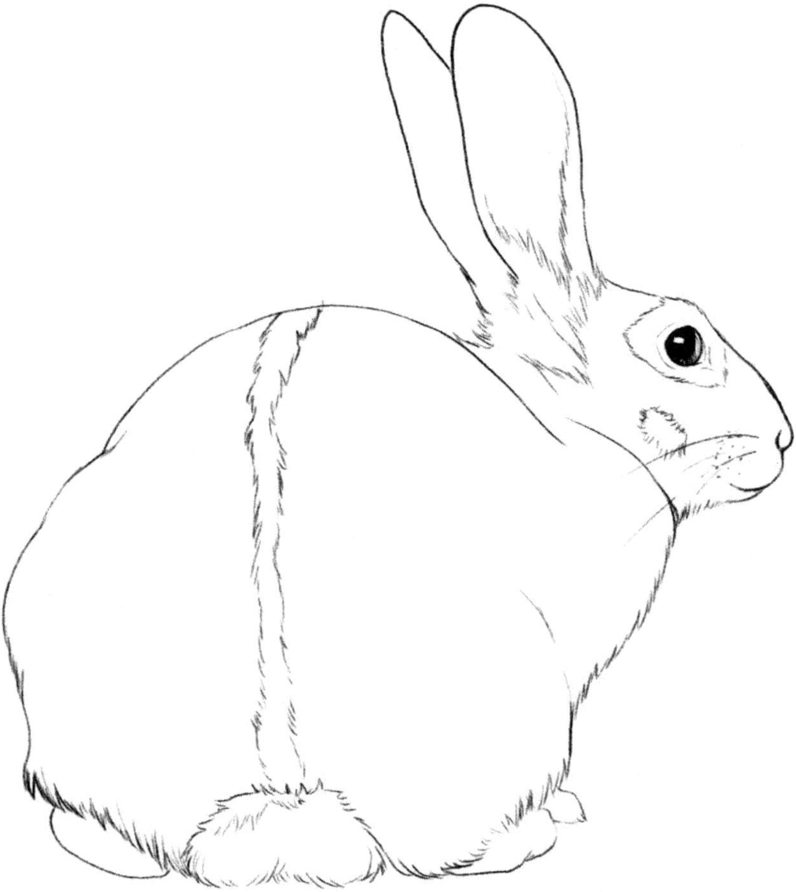

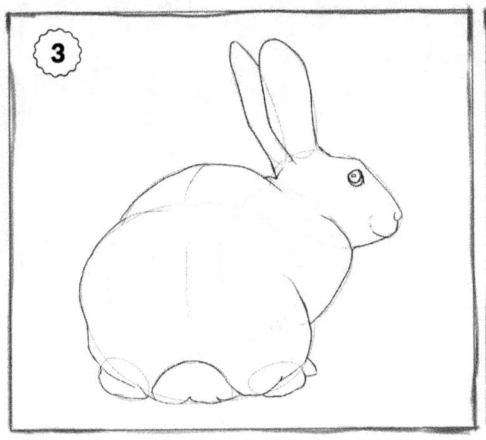
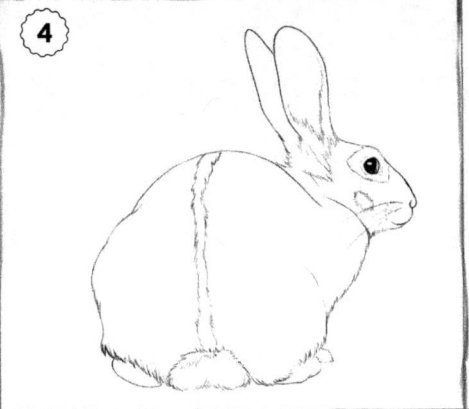

Your turn!

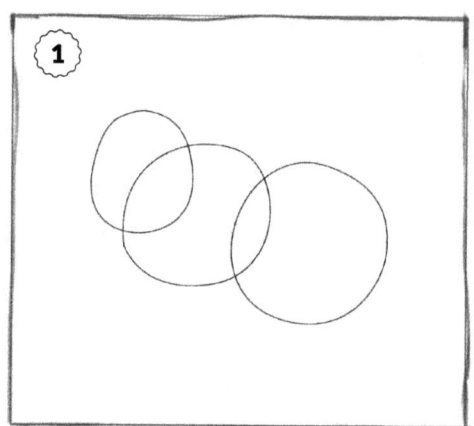
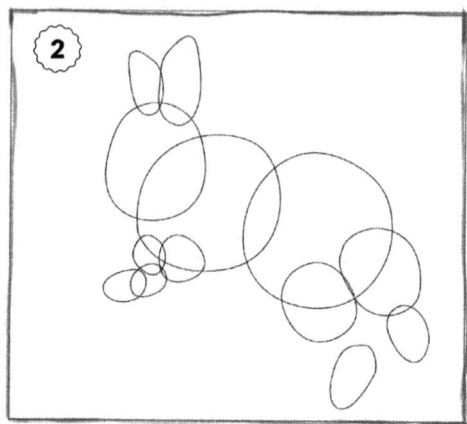

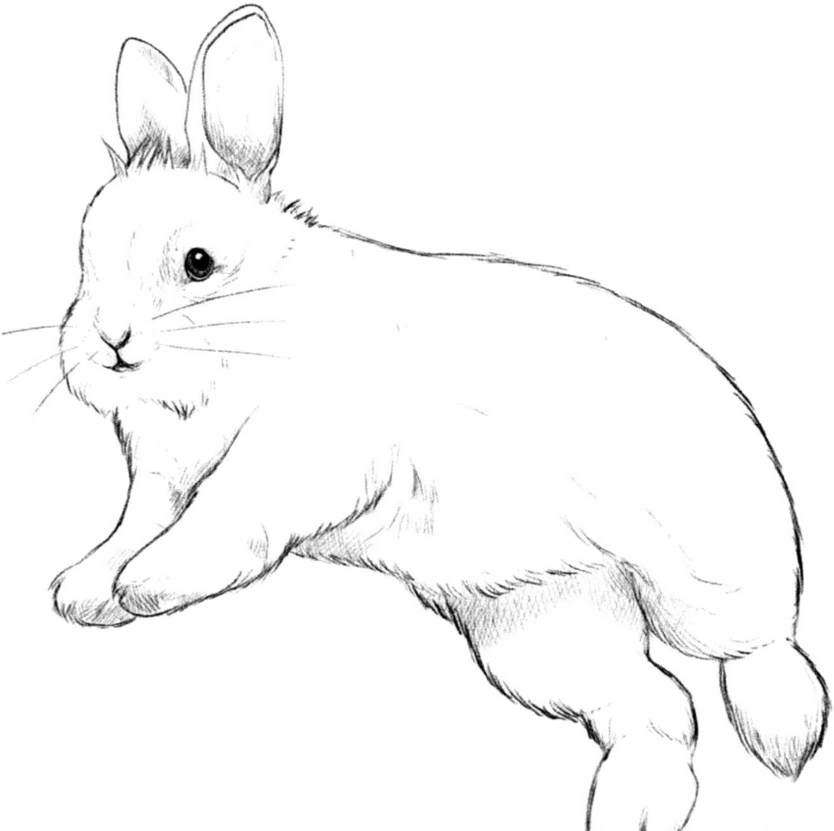

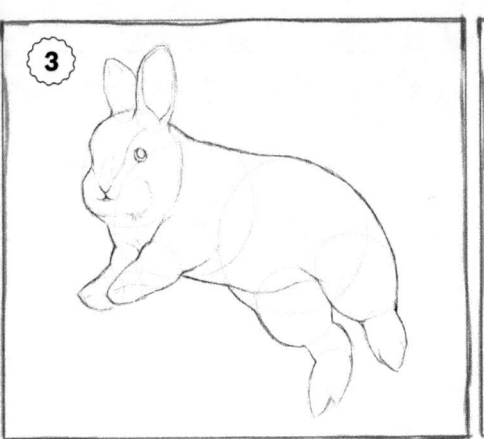 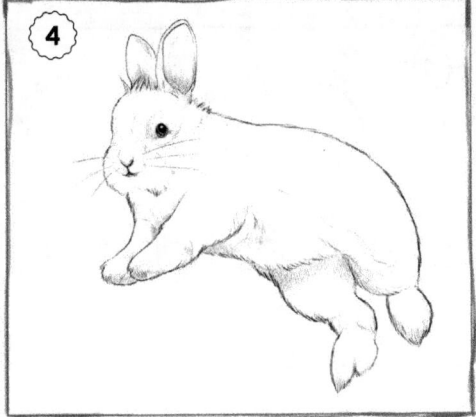

Your turn!

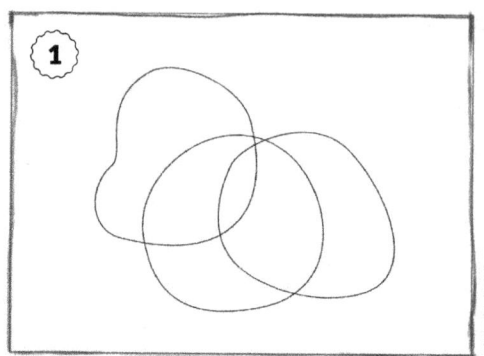 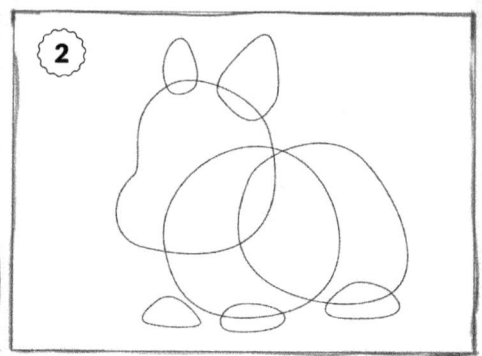

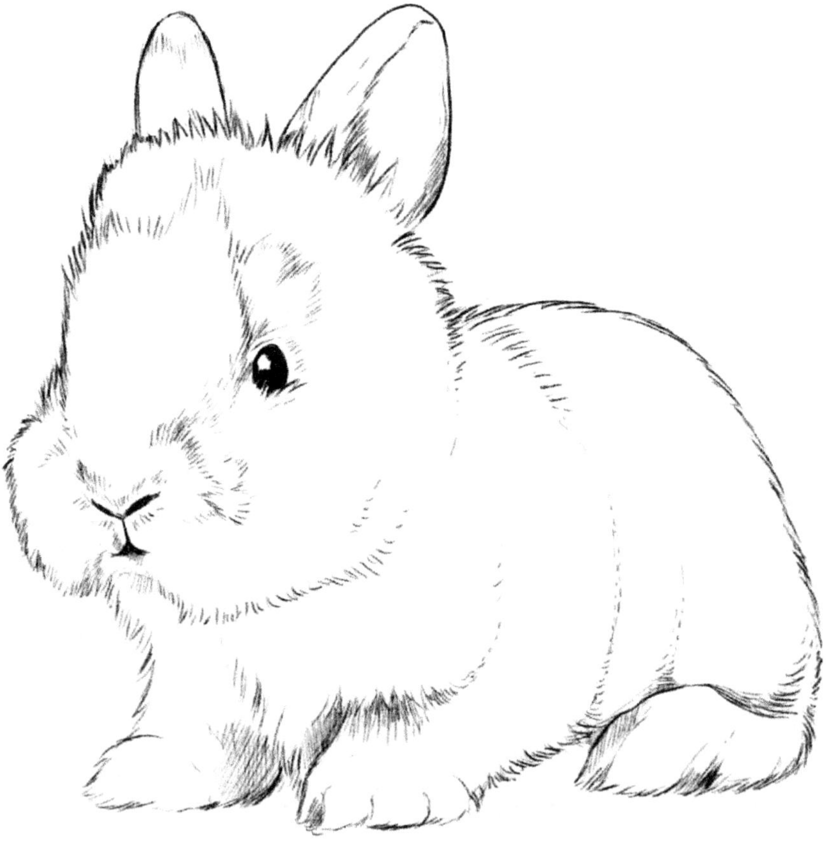

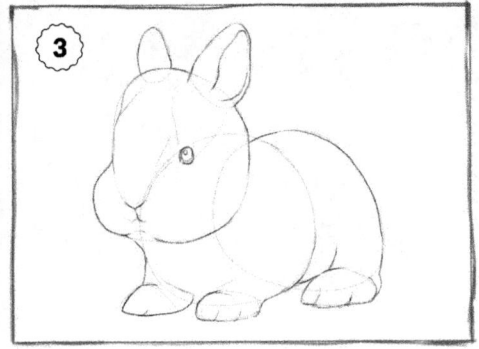
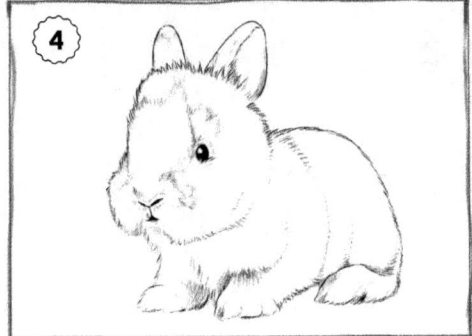

Your turn!

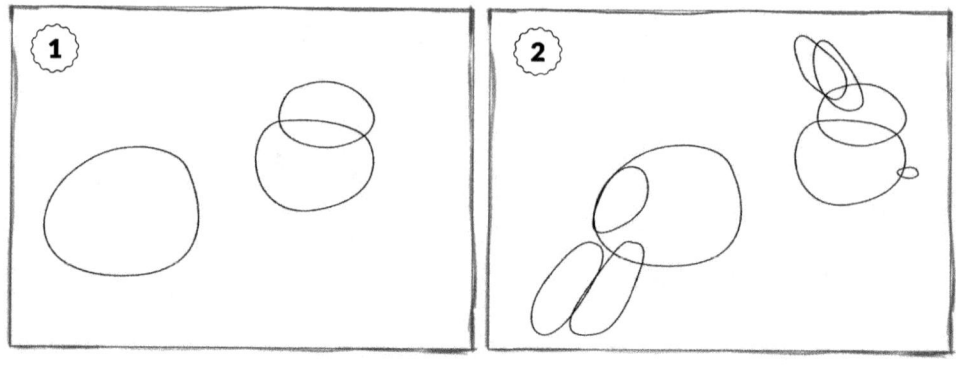

52

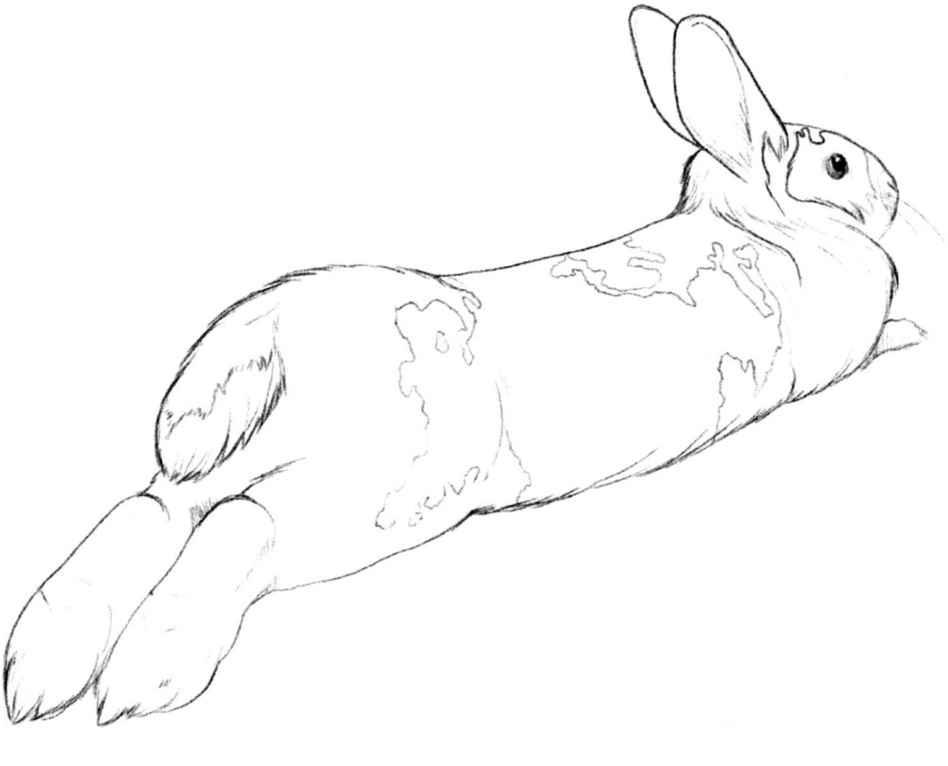

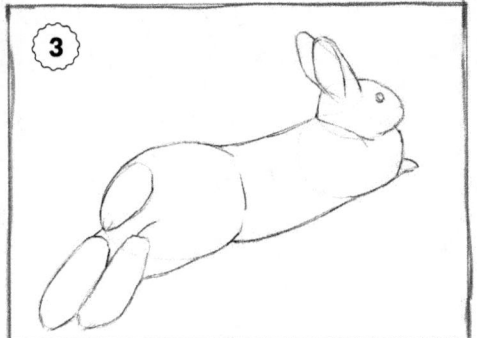
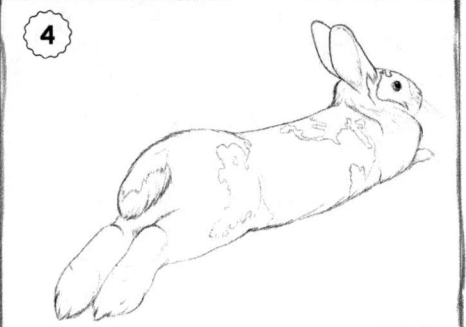

Your turn!

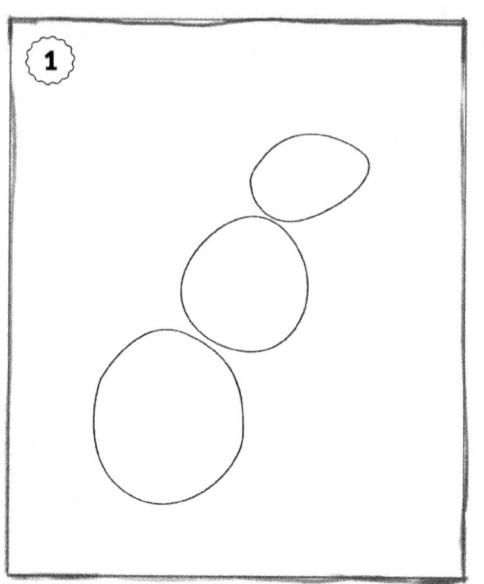
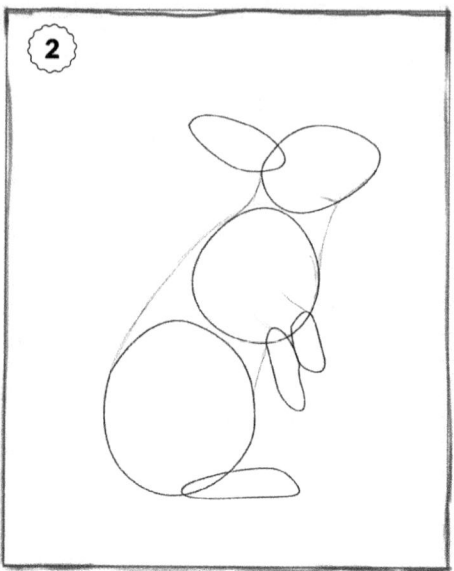
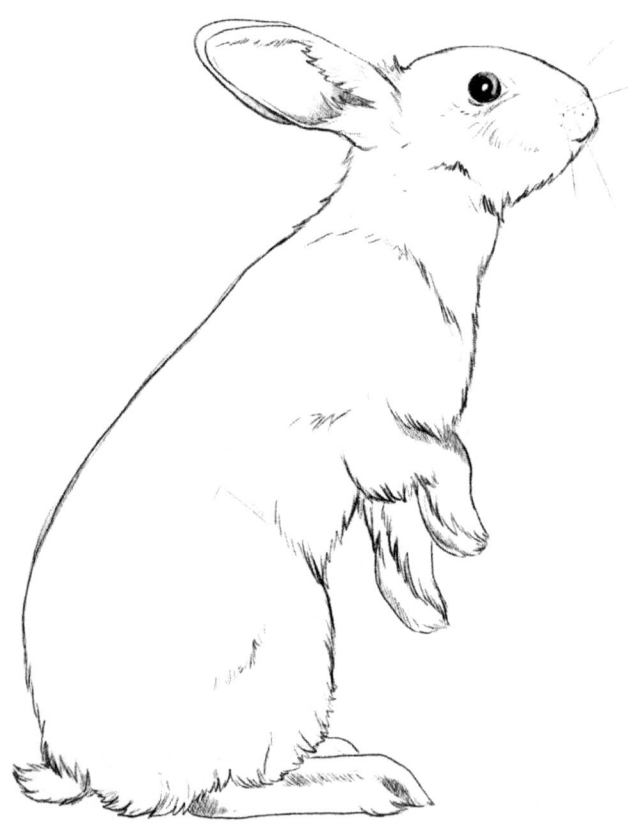

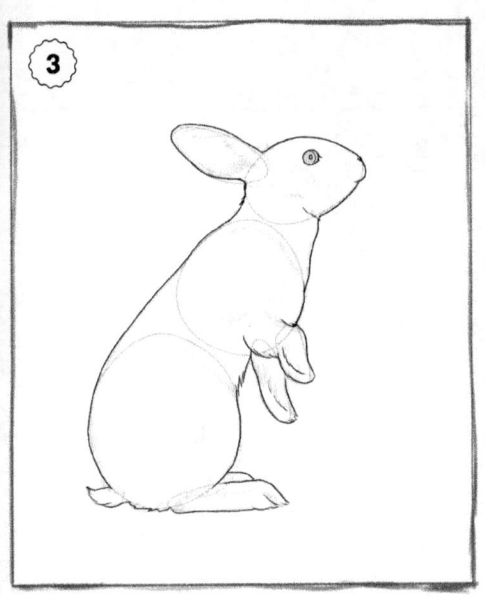
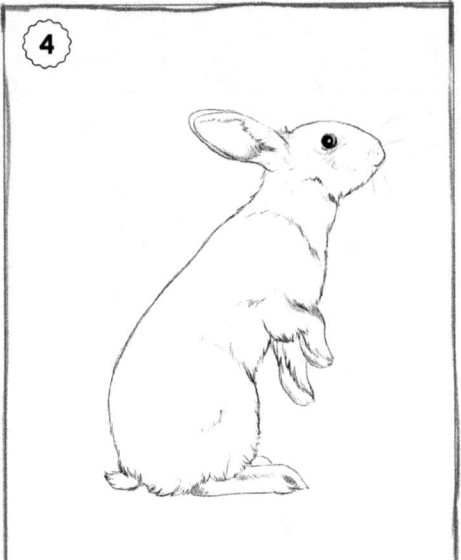

Your turn!

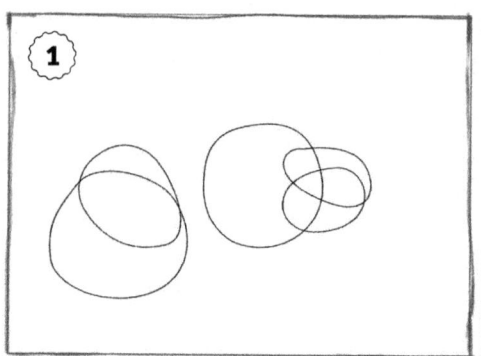
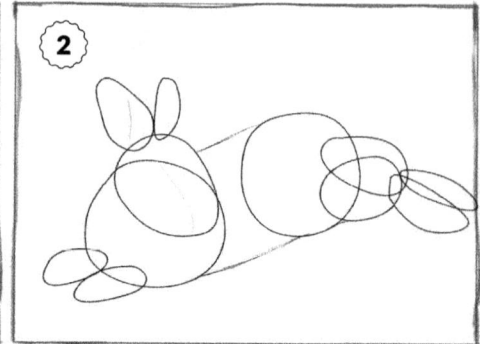
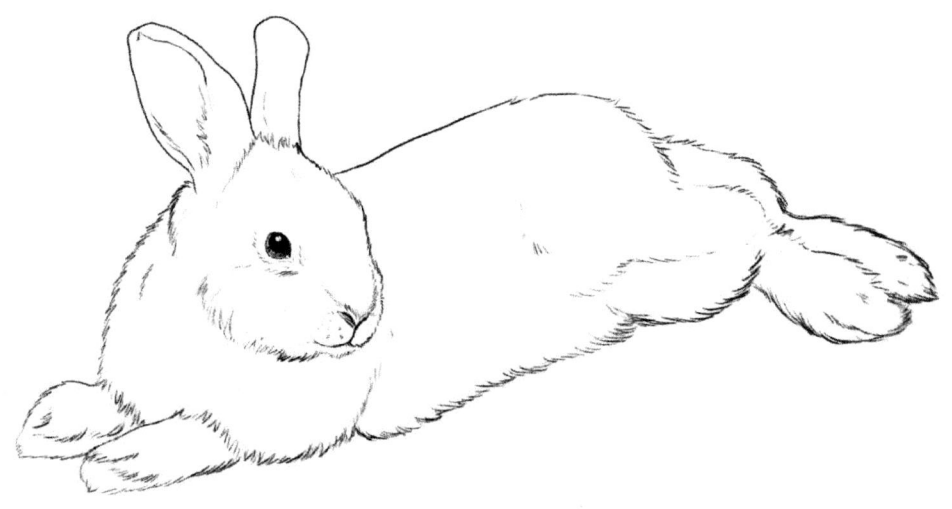

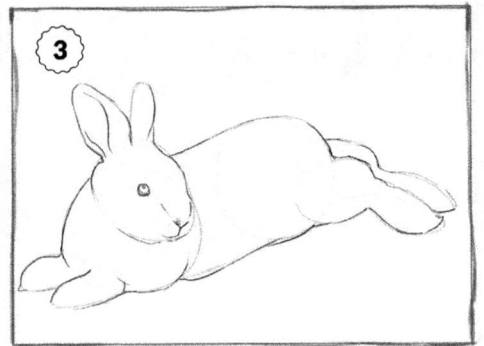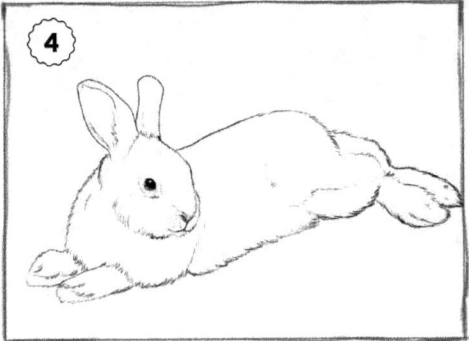

Your turn!

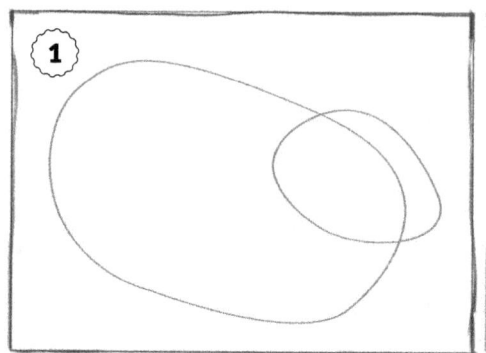
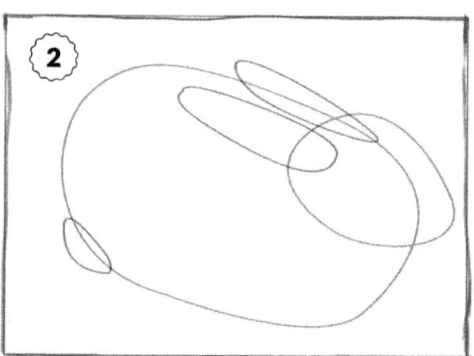
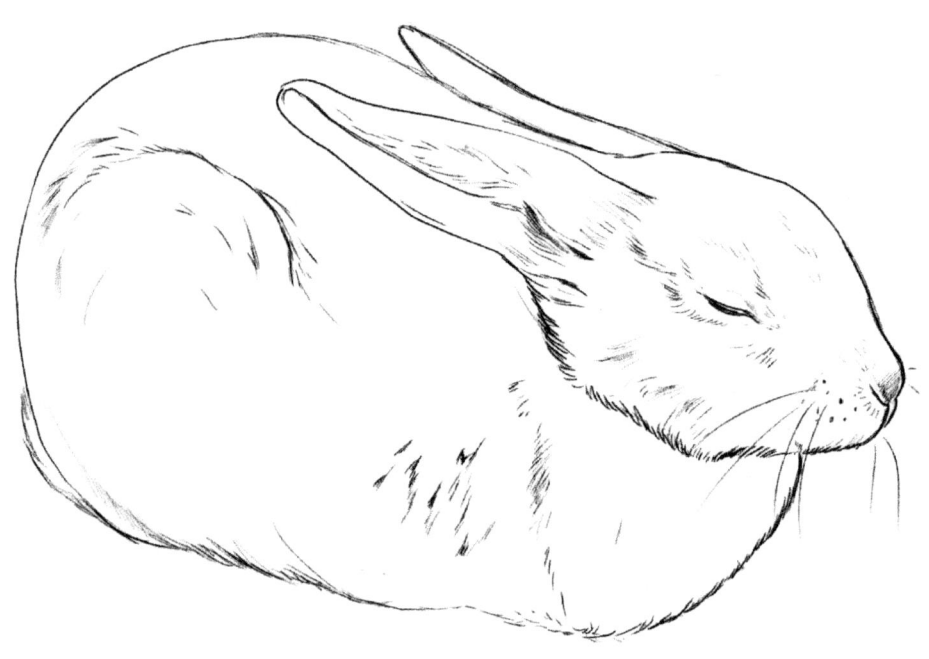

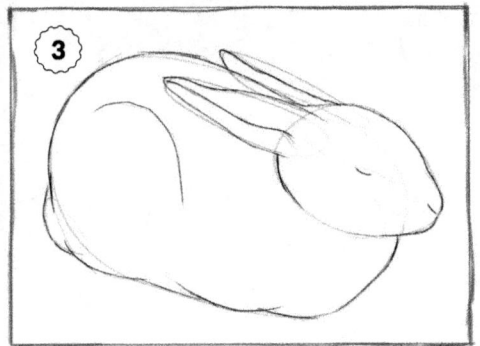
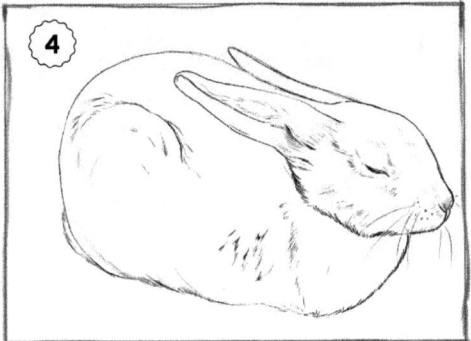

Your turn!

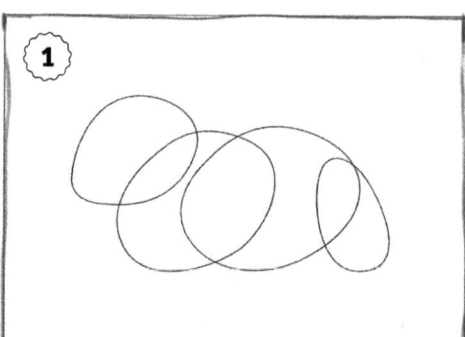
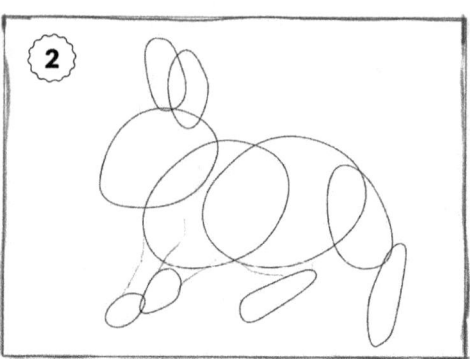

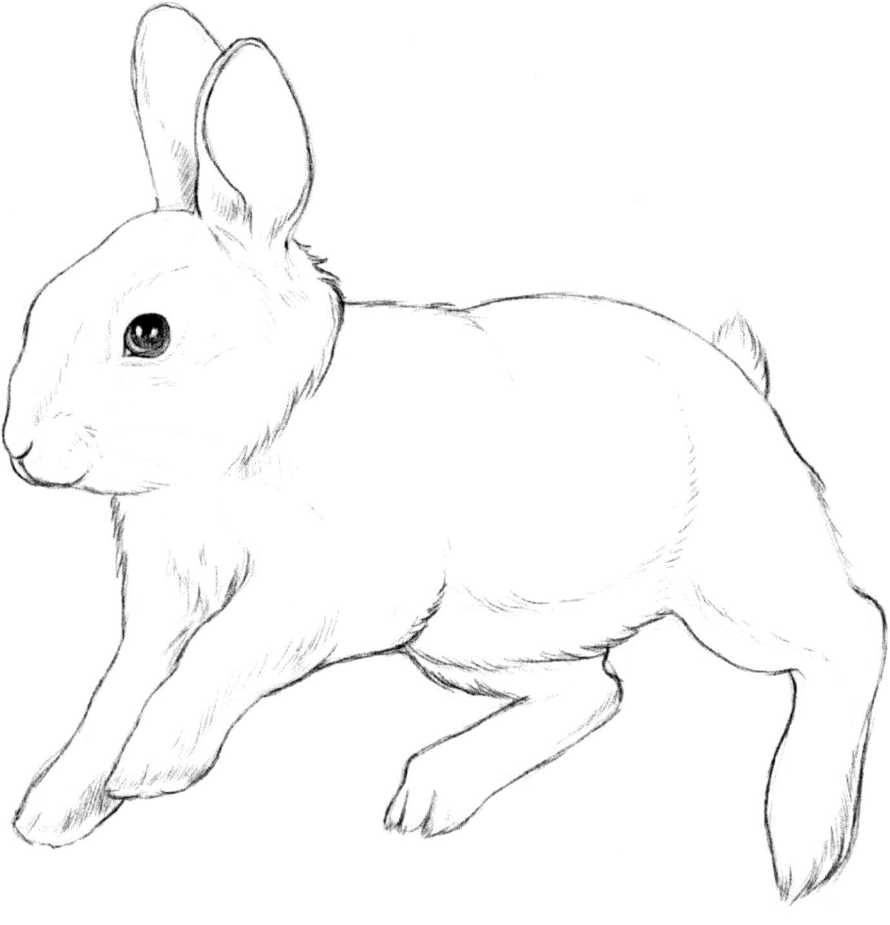

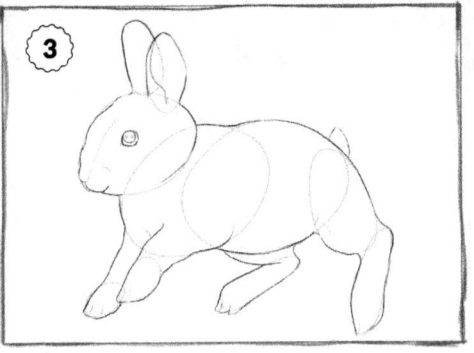
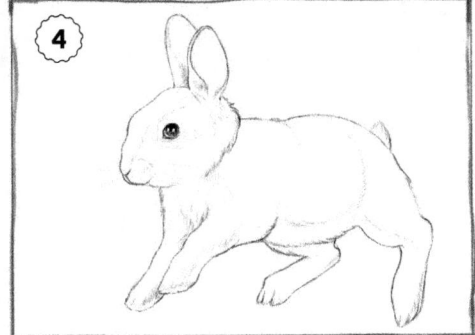

Your turn!

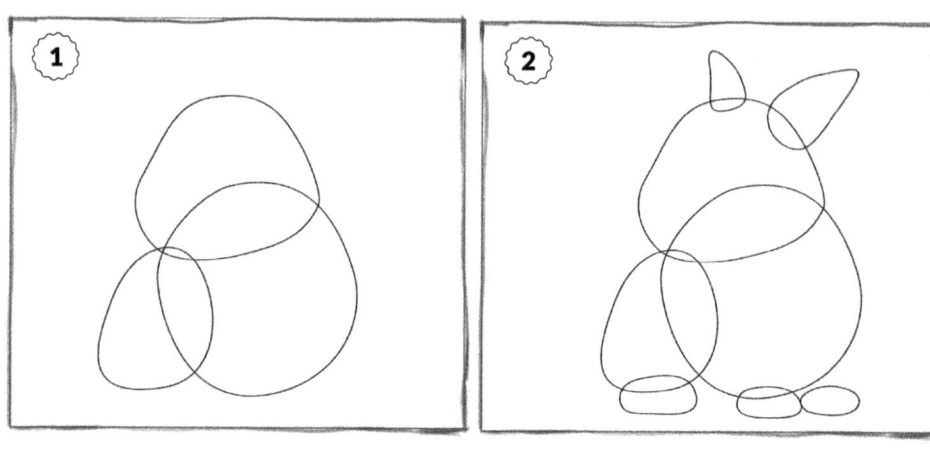

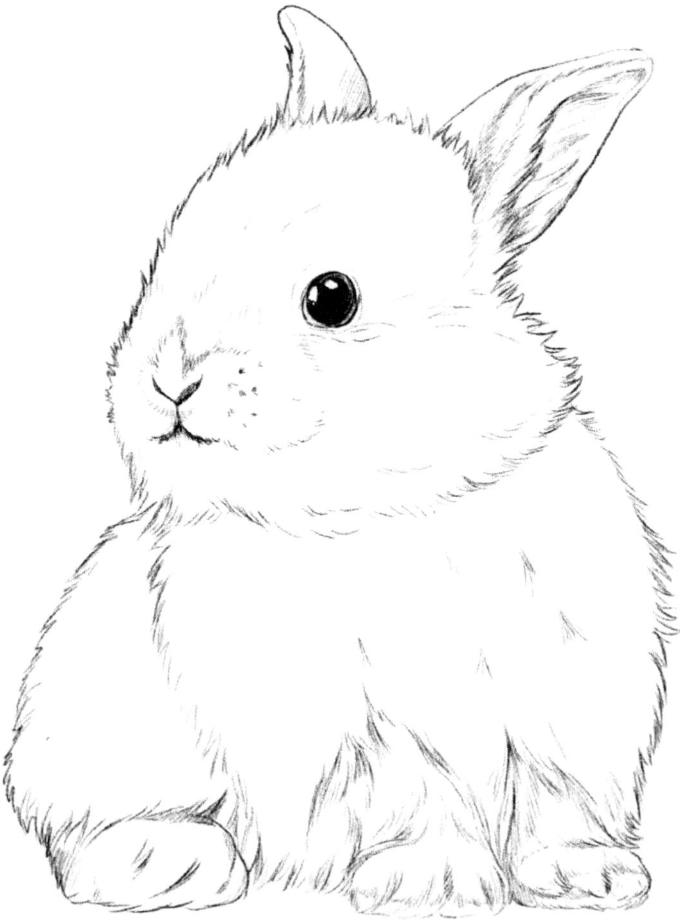

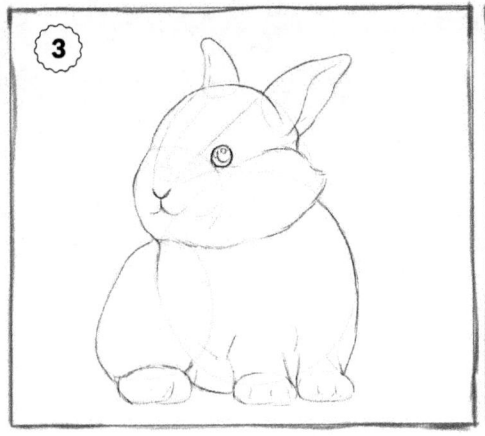
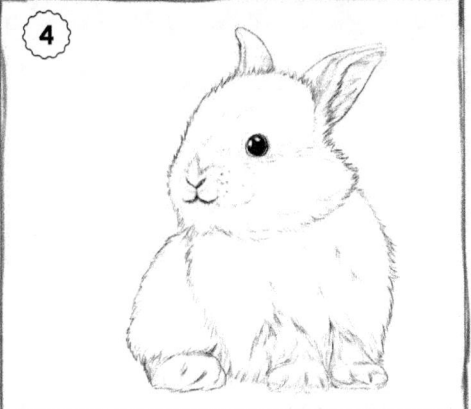

Your turn!

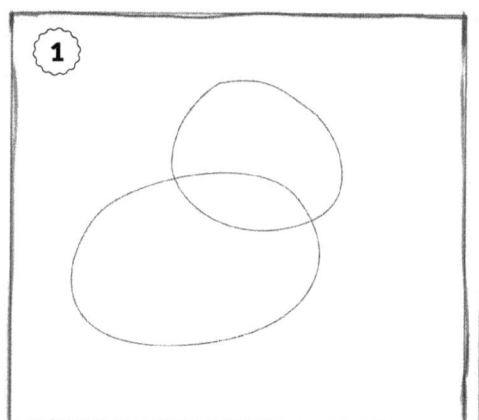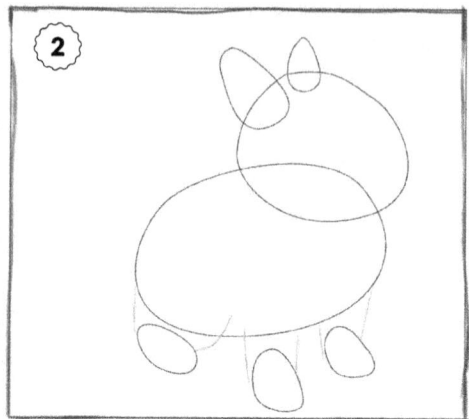

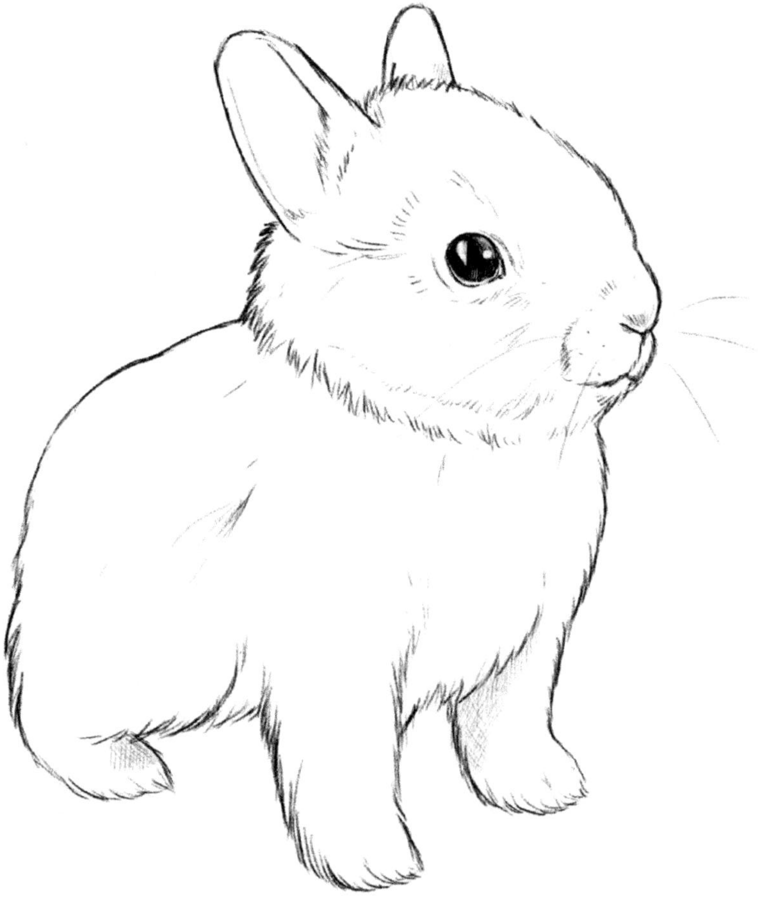

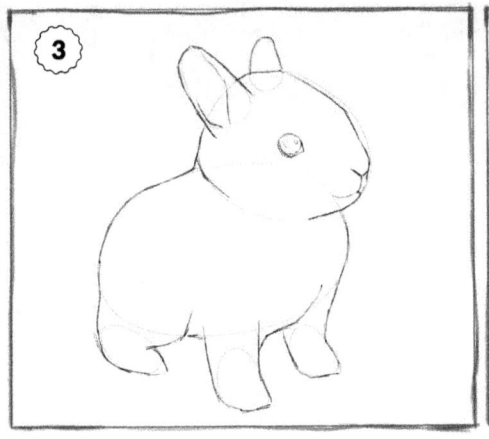
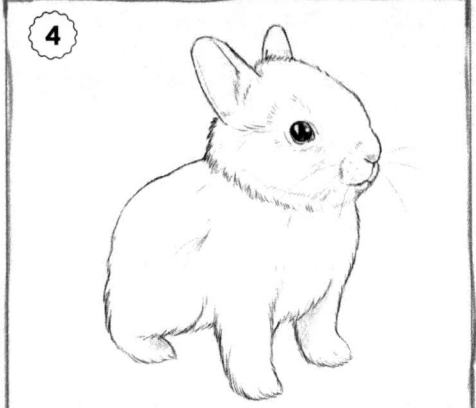

Your turn!

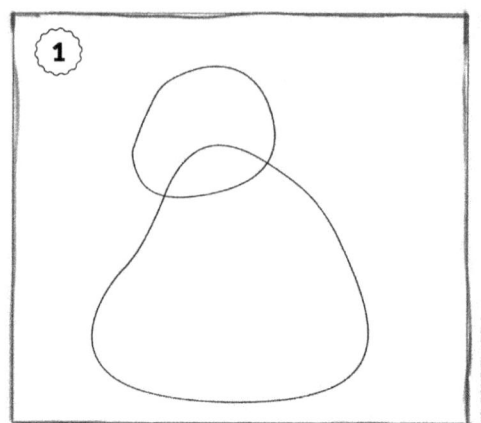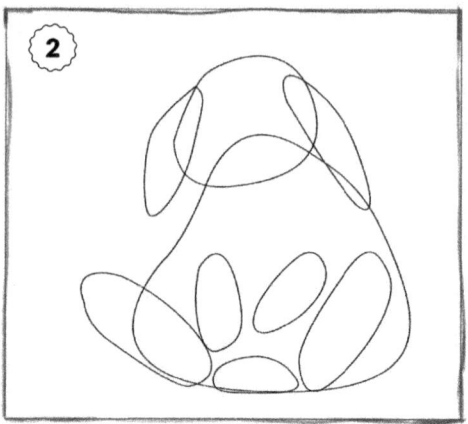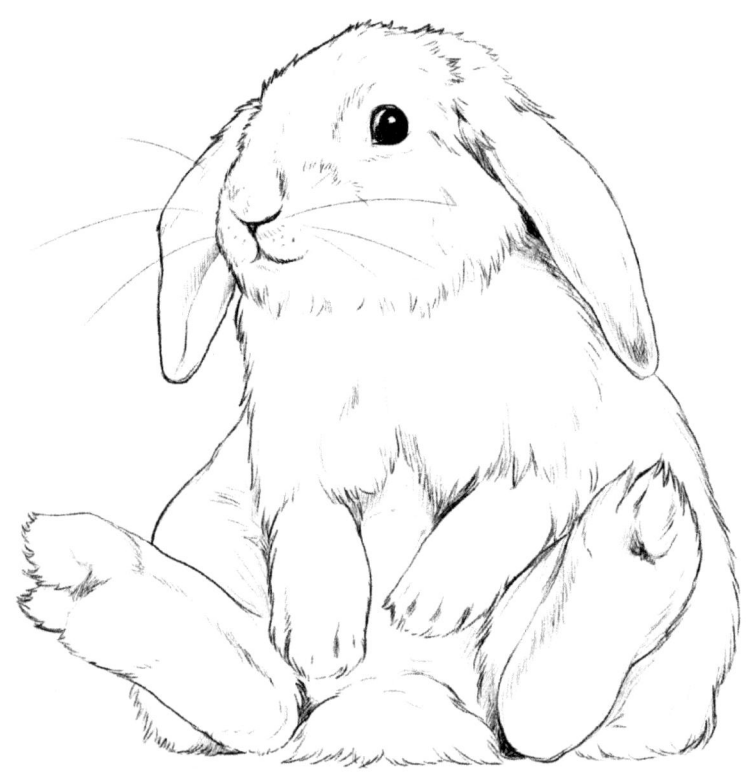

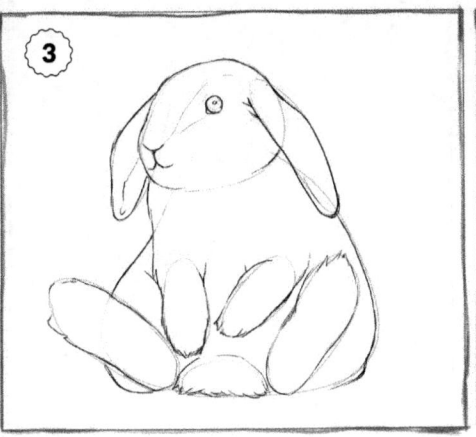
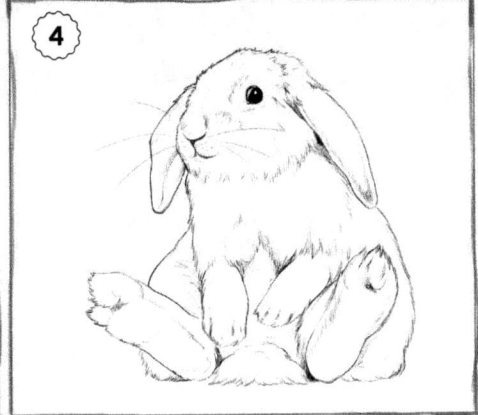

Your turn!

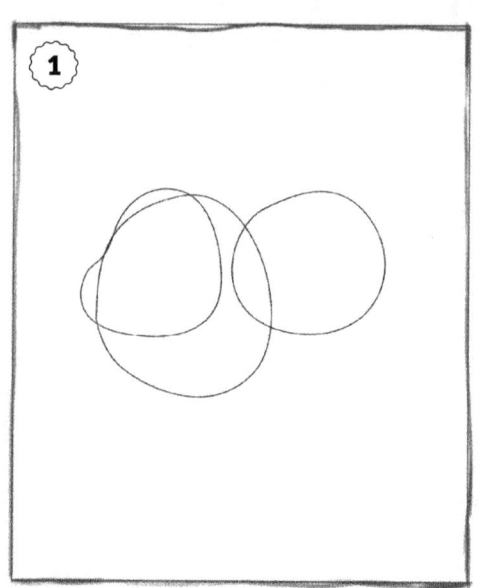
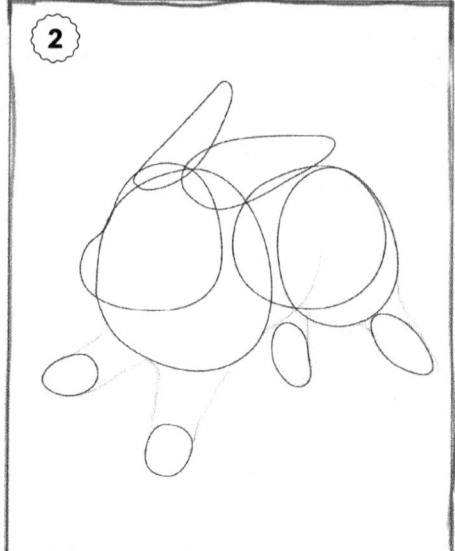

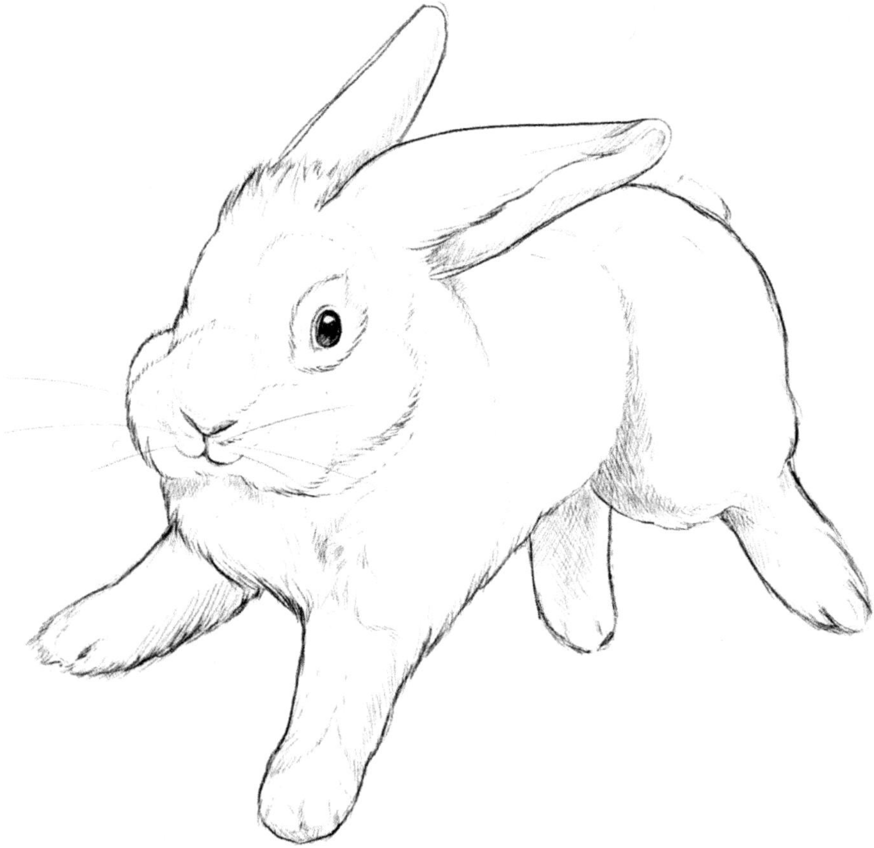

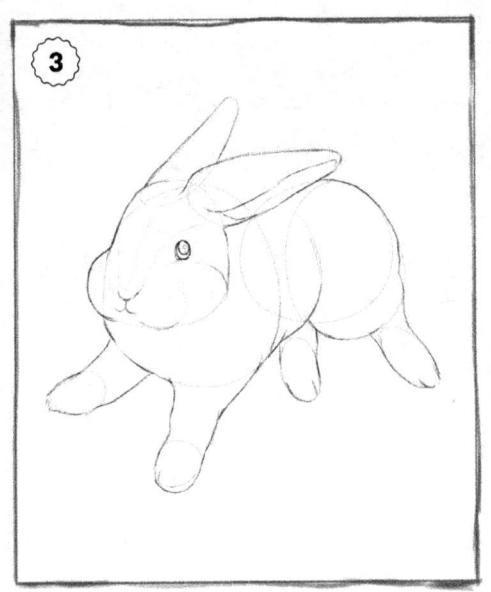
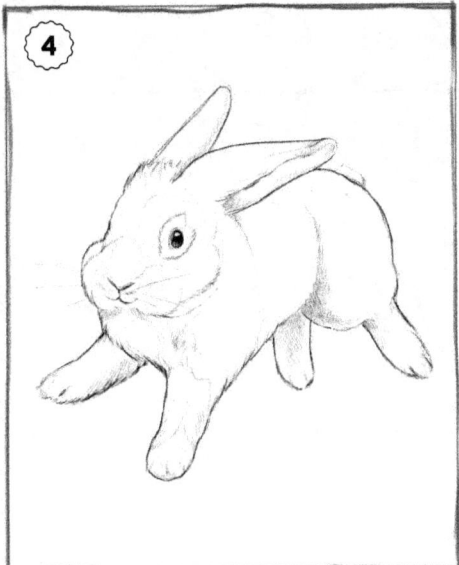

Your turn!

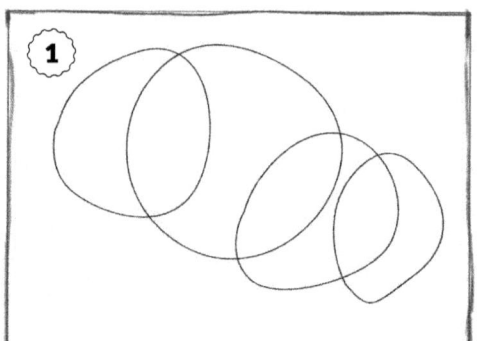
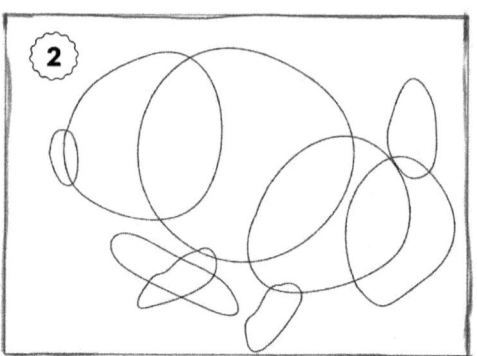

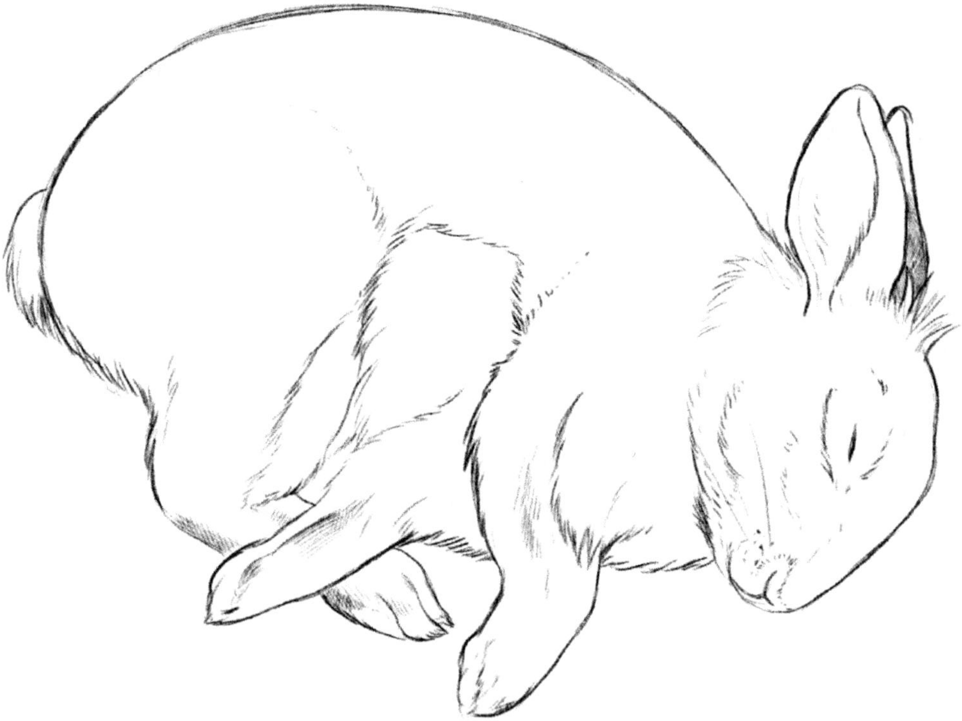

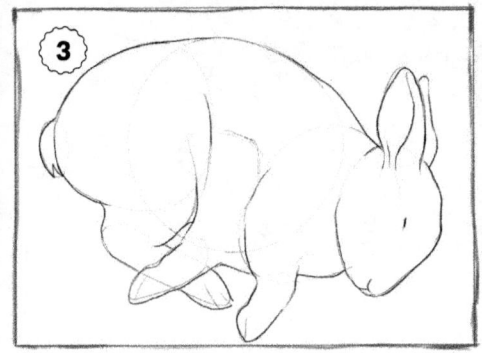
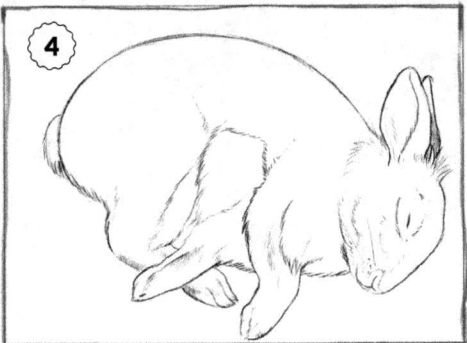

Your turn!

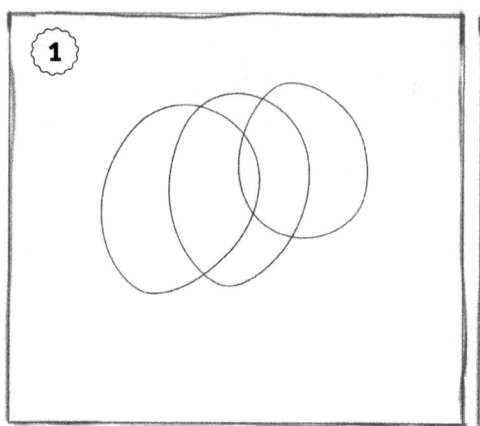
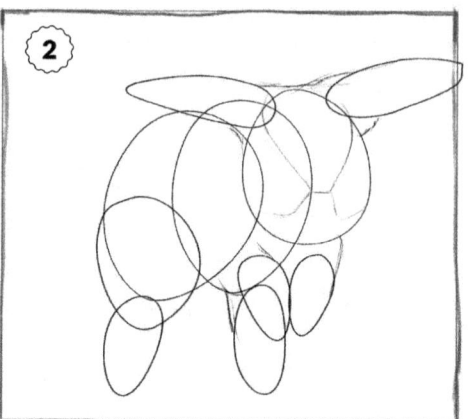
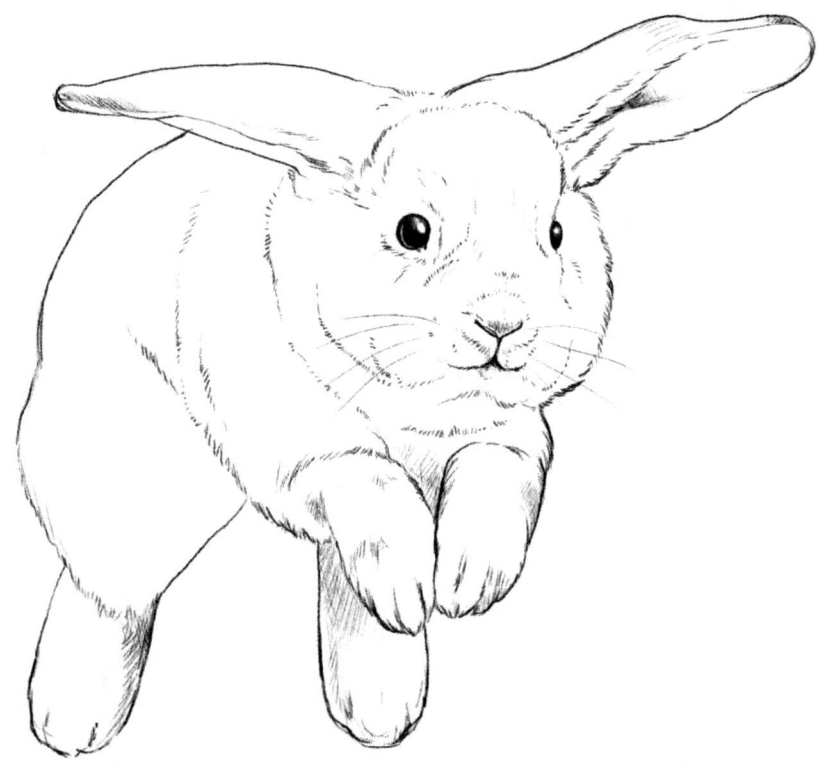

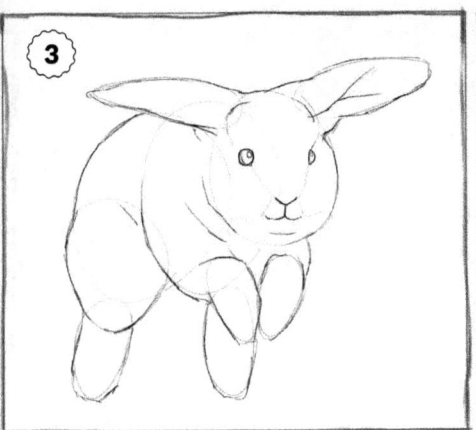
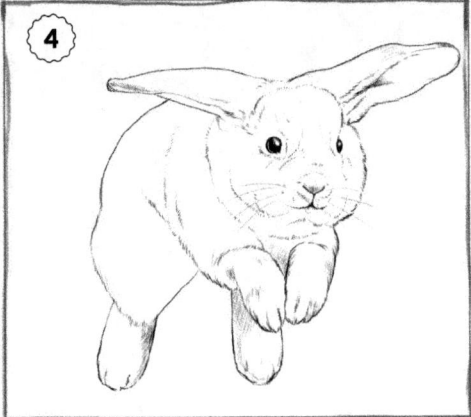

Your turn!

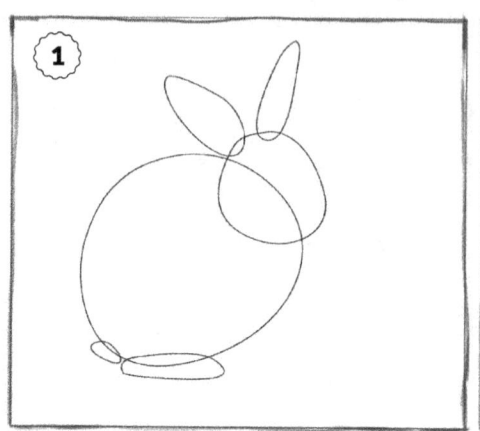
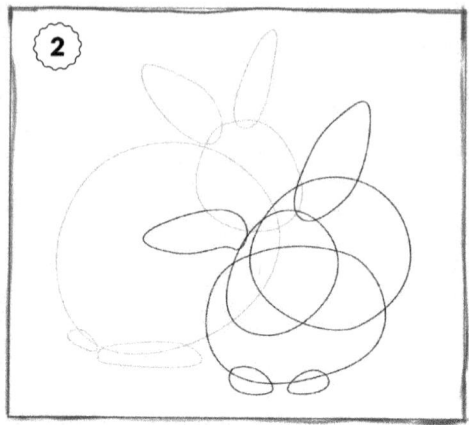

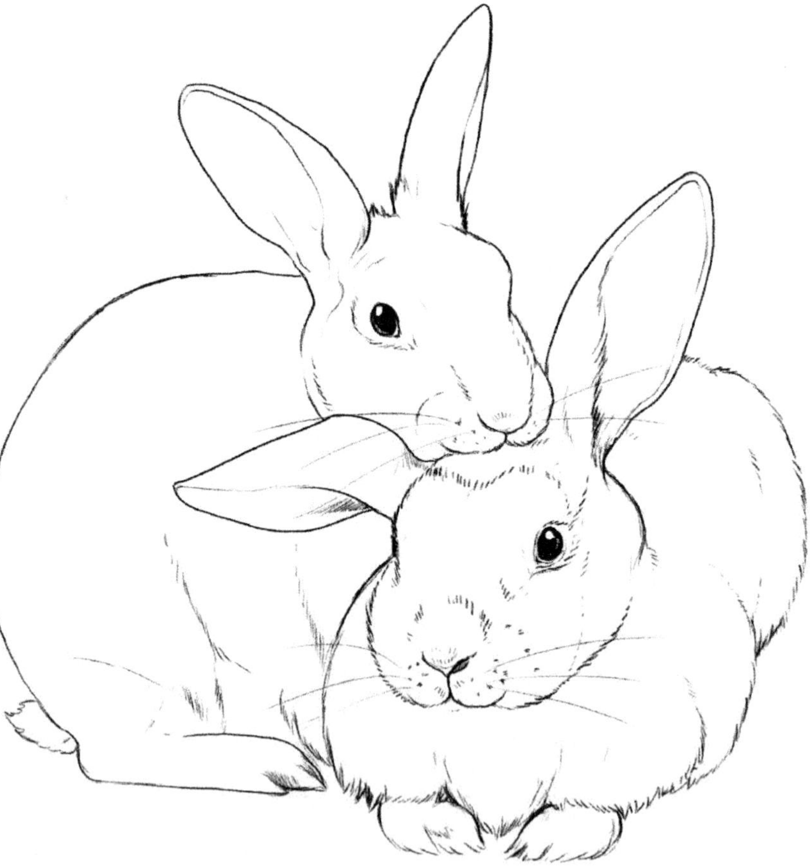

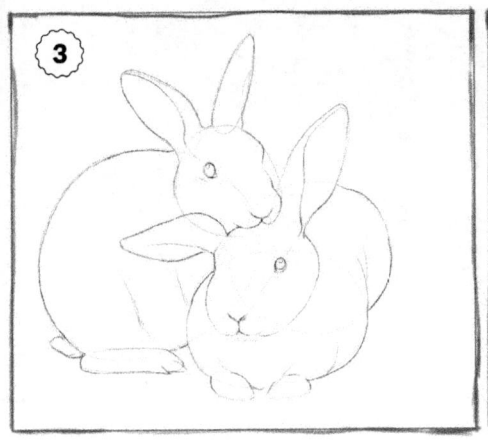
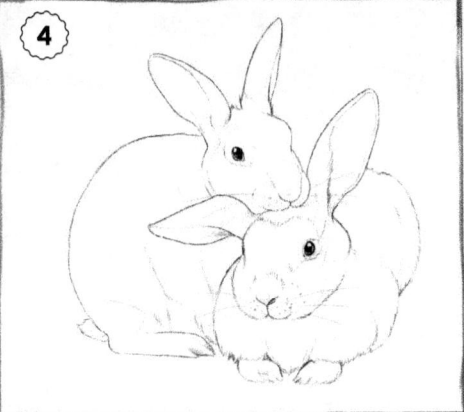

Your turn!

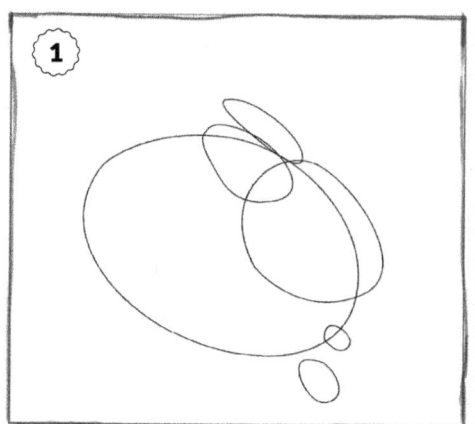
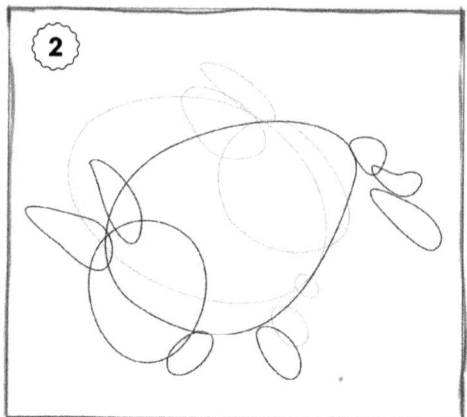

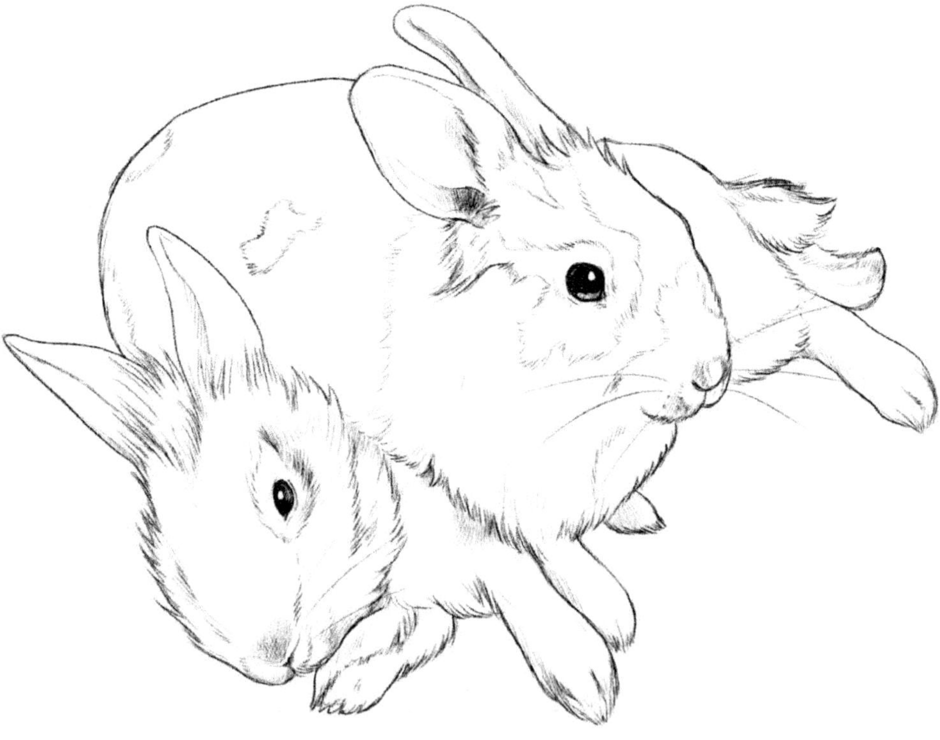

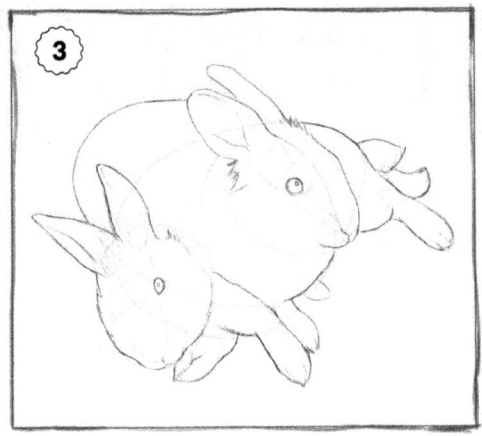
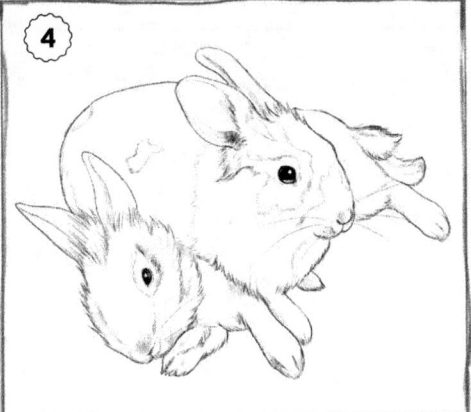

Your turn!

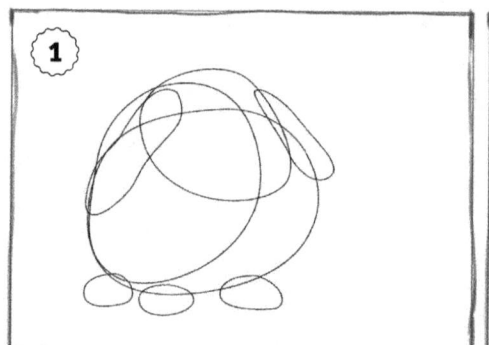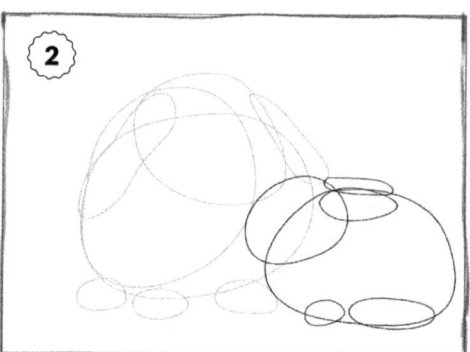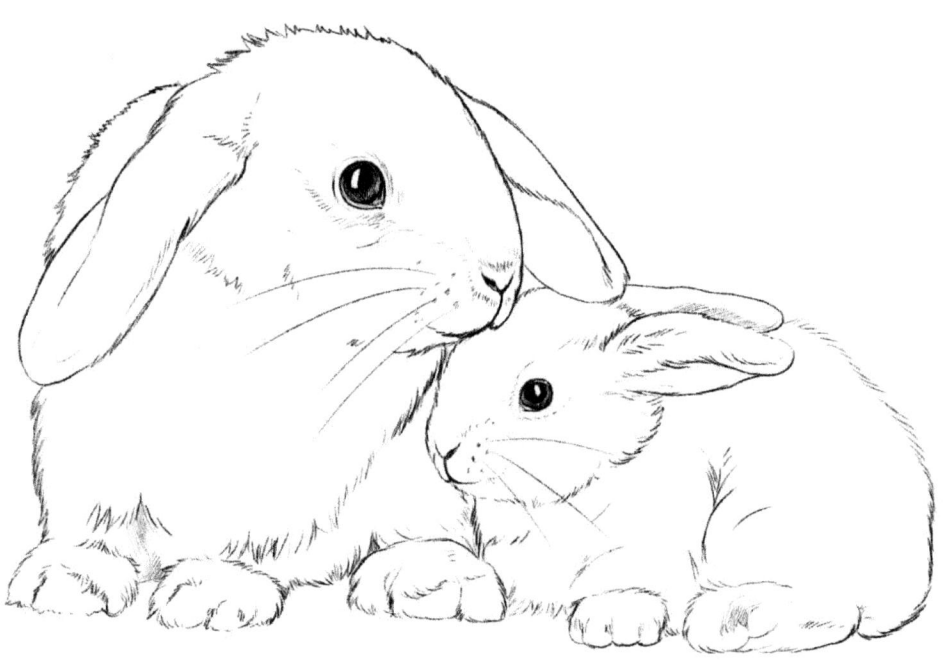

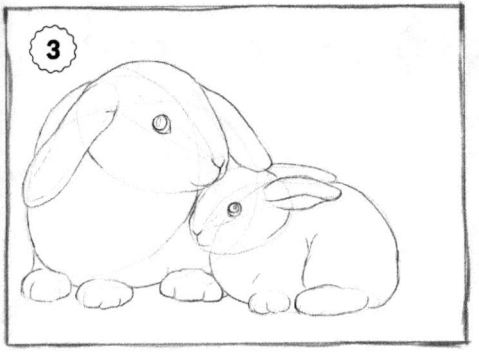
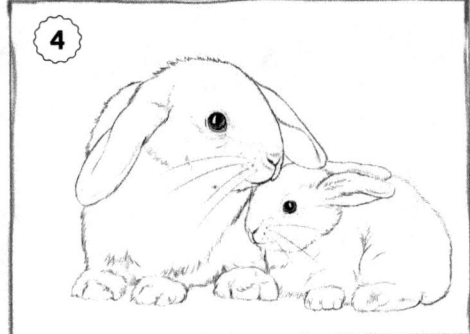

Your turn!

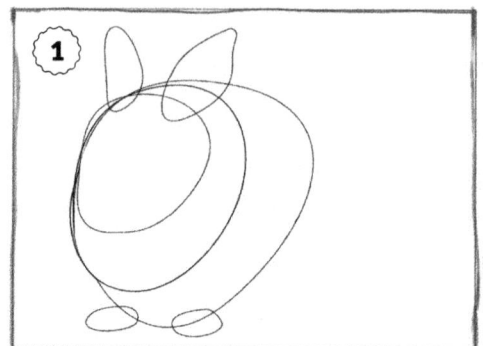
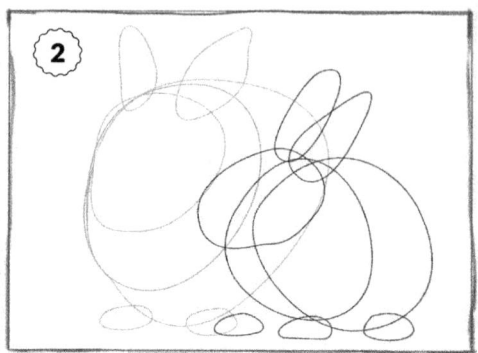

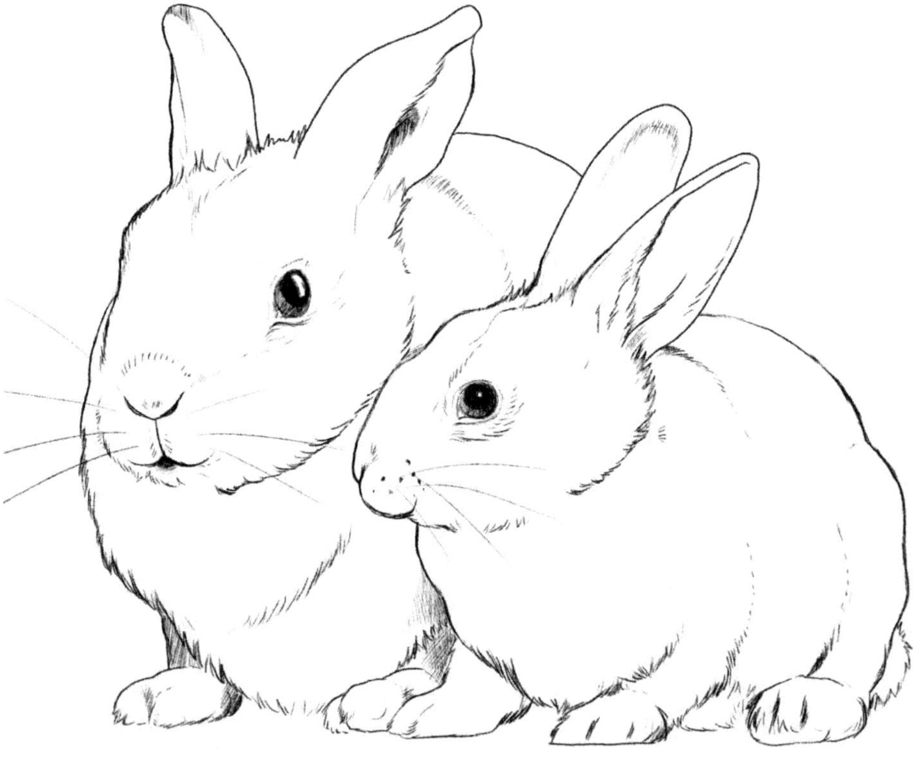

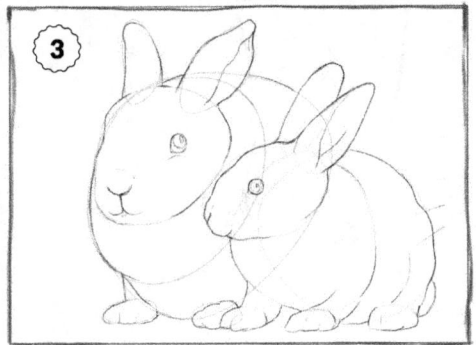
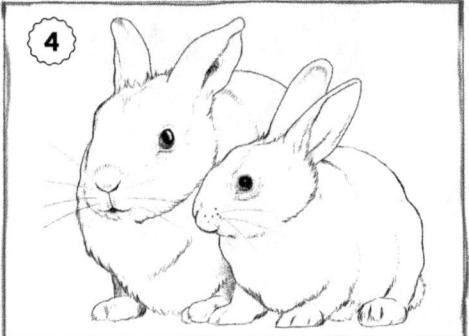

Your turn!

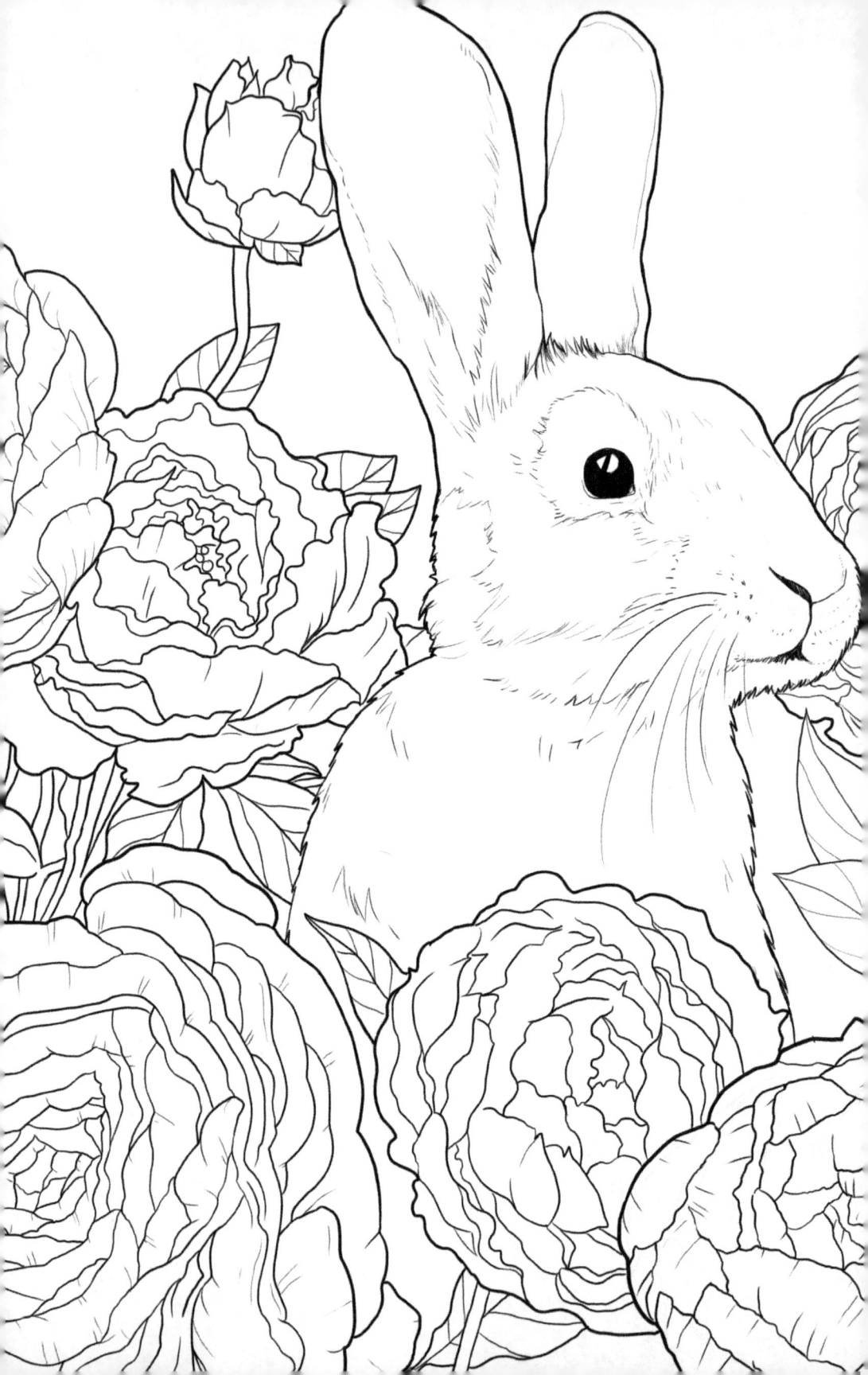

Keep calm and love your Bunnies

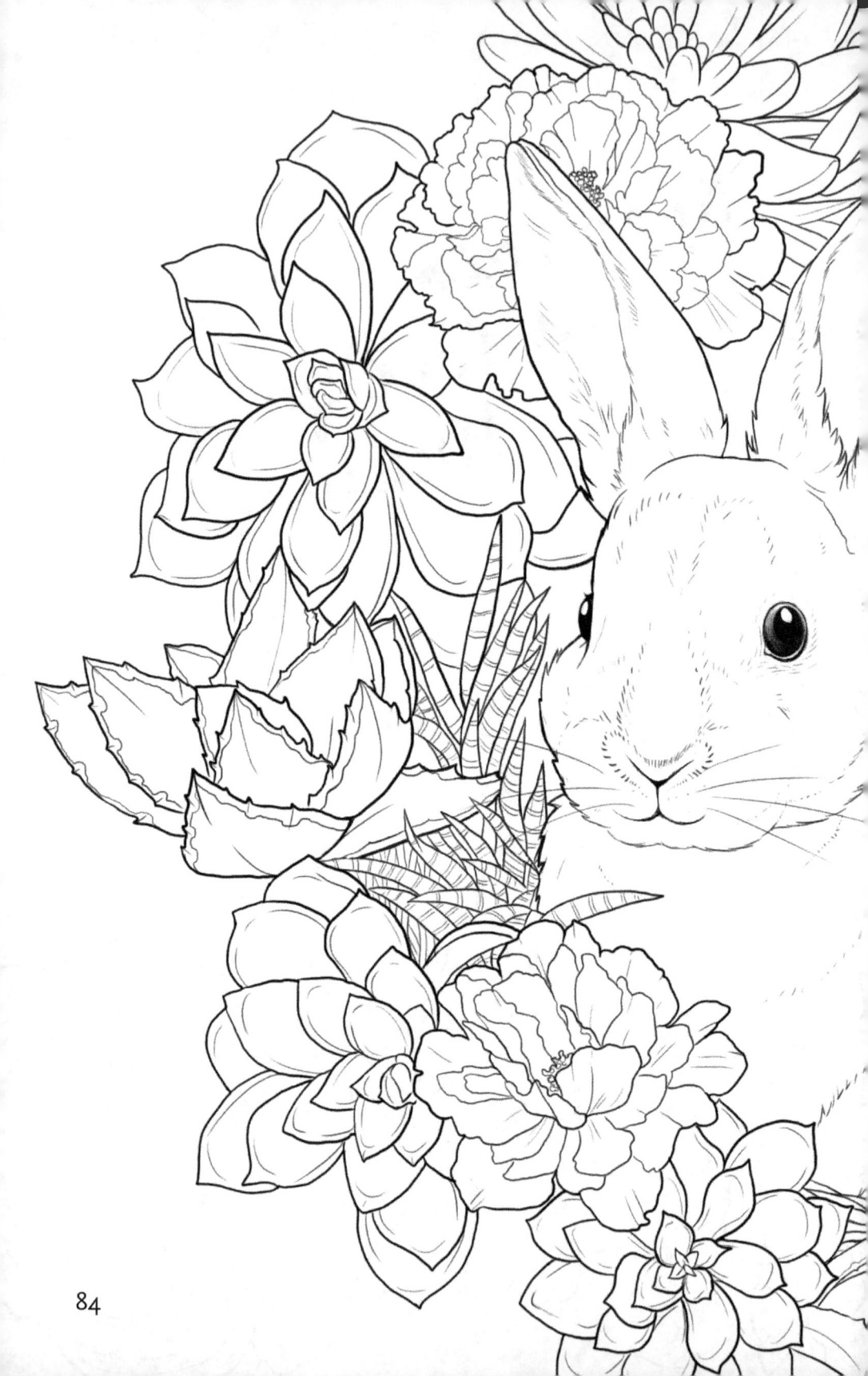

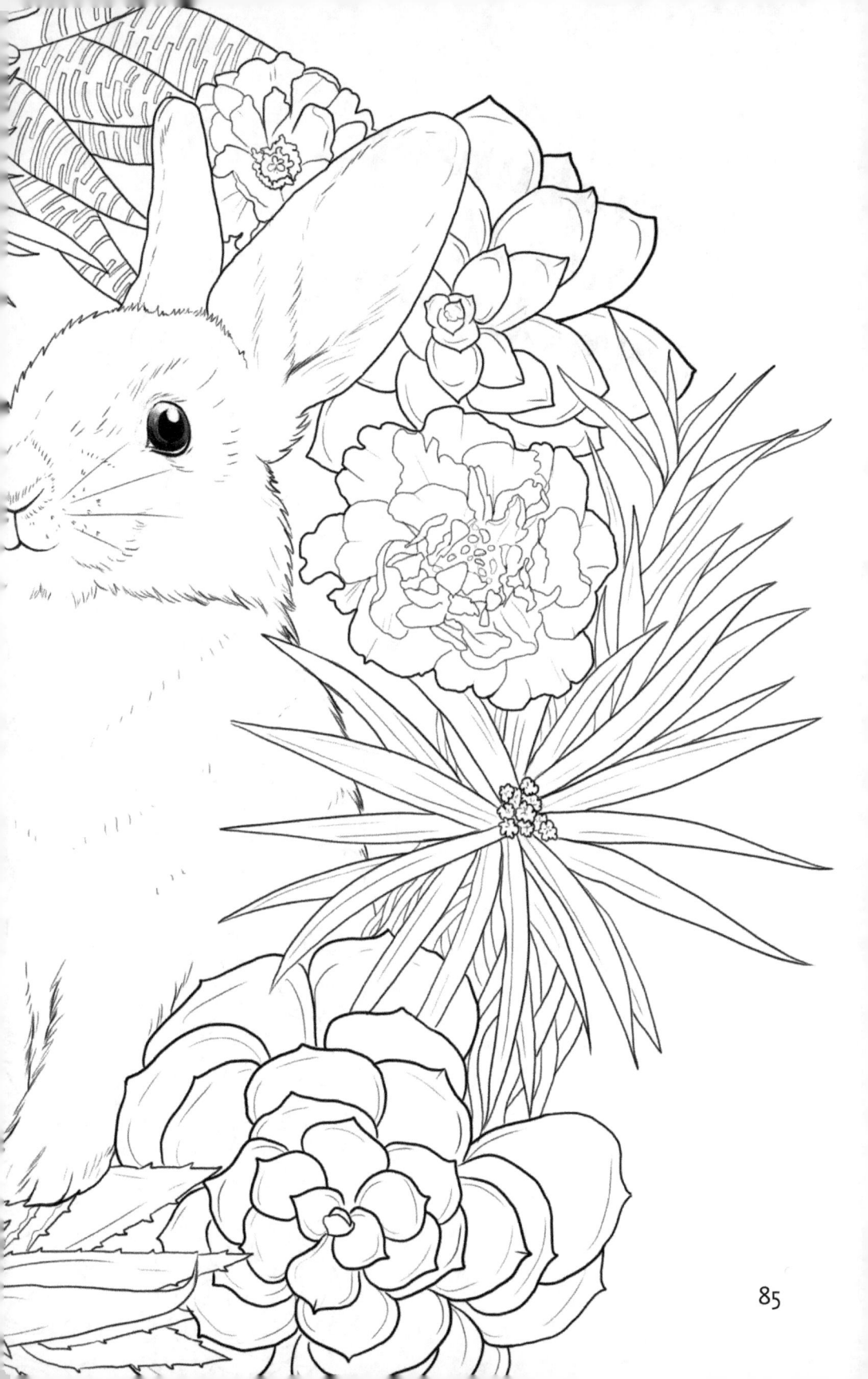

Everybunny needs somebunny

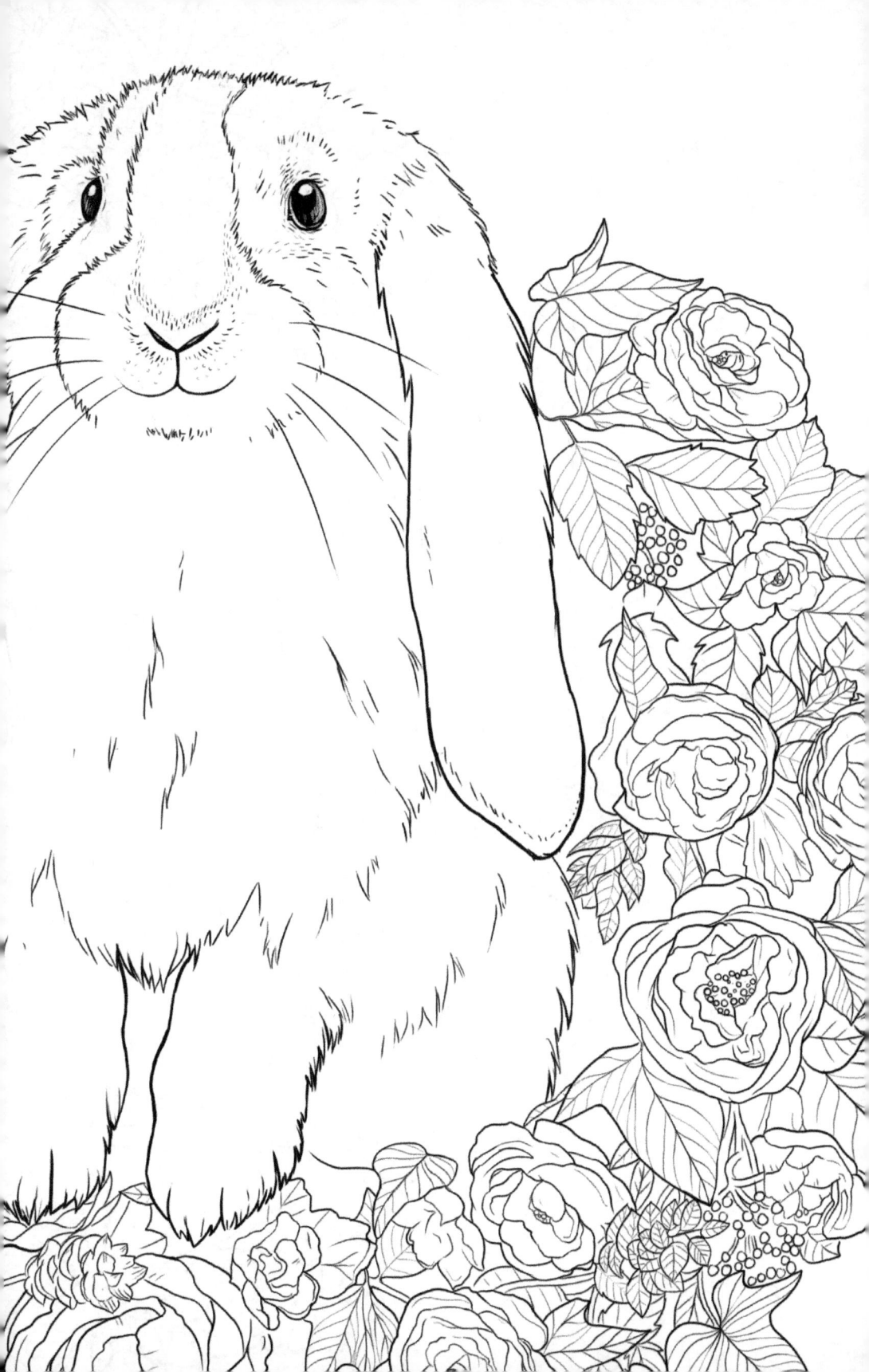

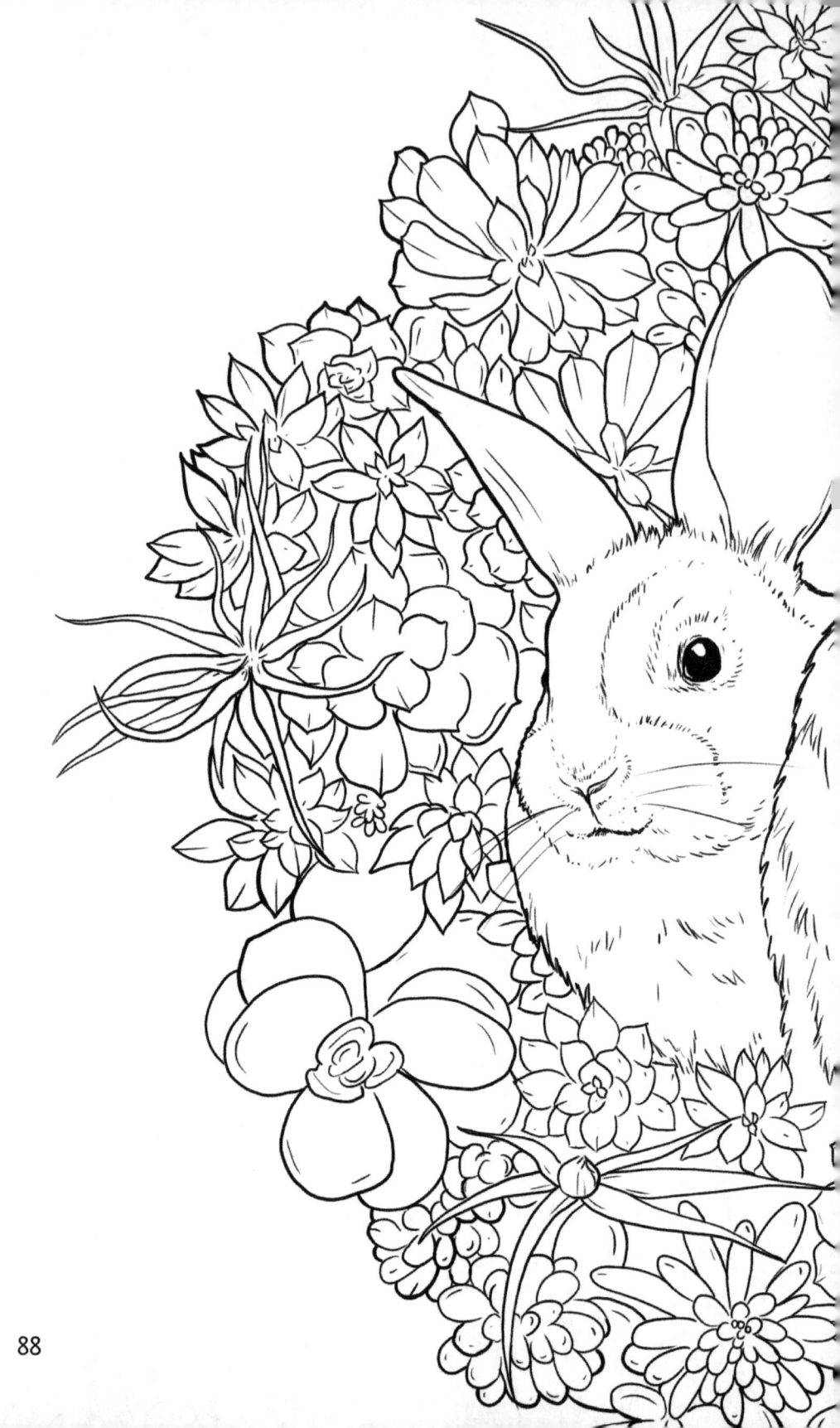

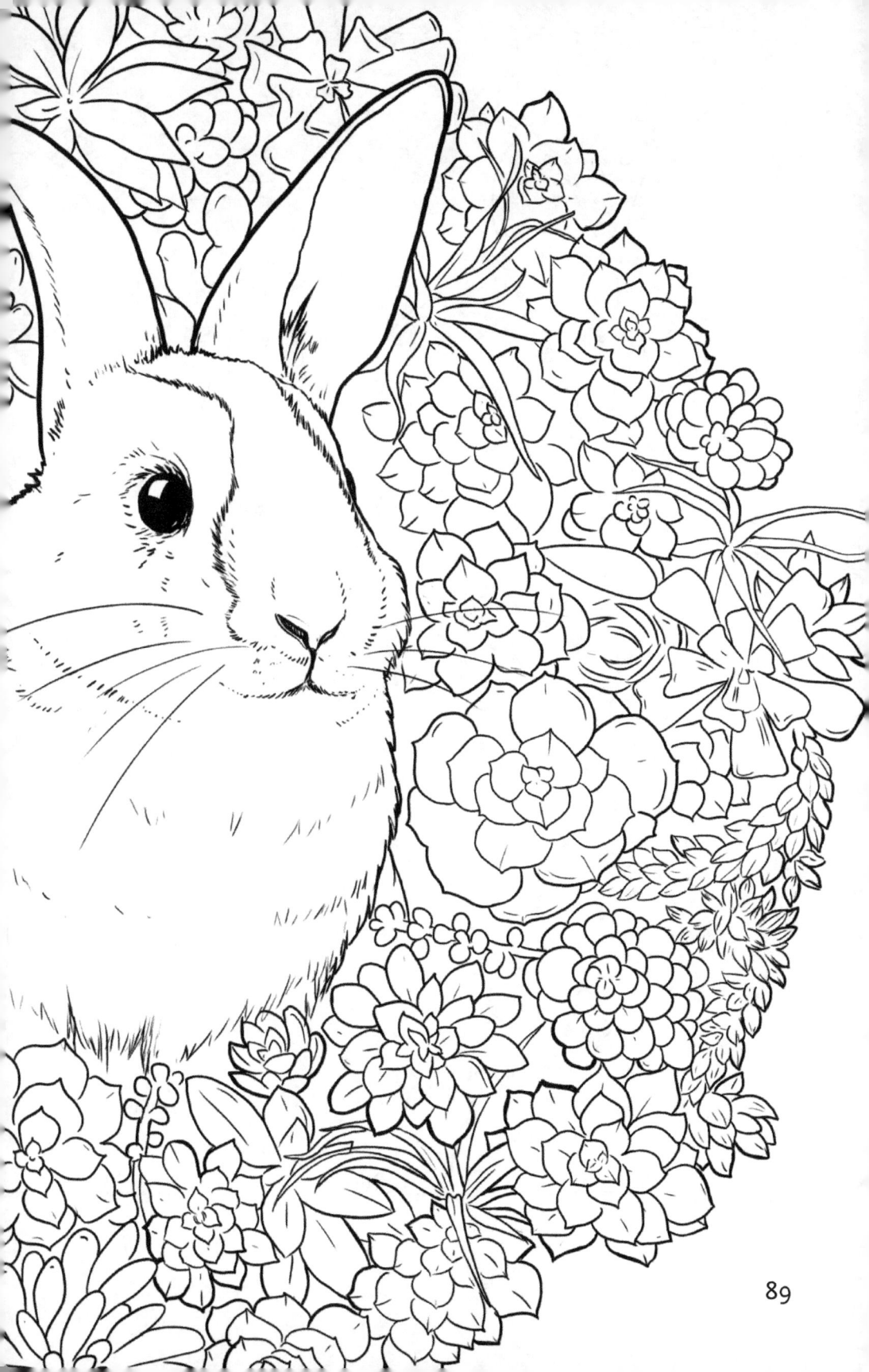

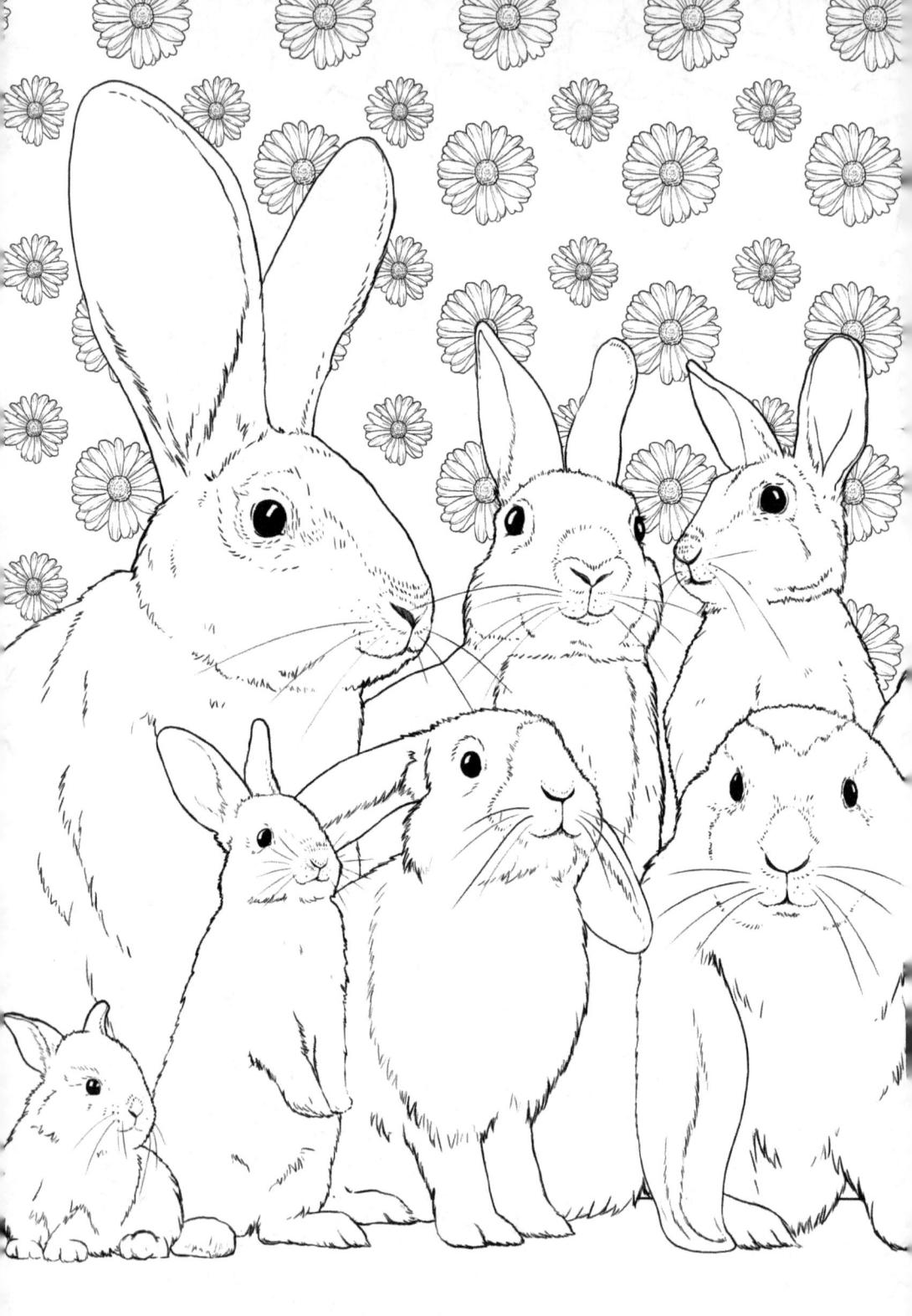

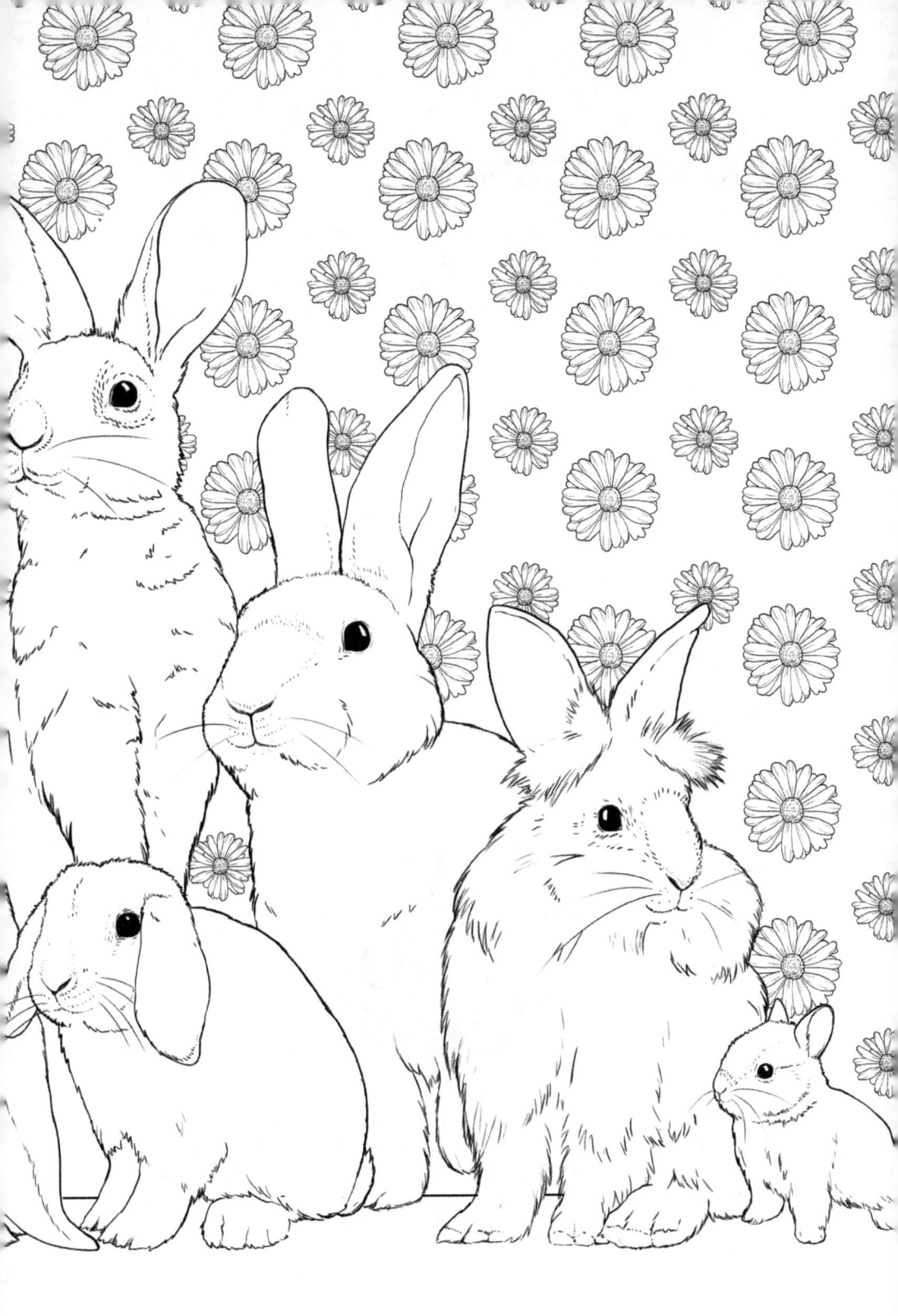

ACKNOWLEDGMENTS

A big thank you to my good friend Ursina who helped me with this project.
Thank you to Andy for always supporting me and holding me accountable.
Thank you to Ragnar and Lagherta, the two whimsical and incredibly cute creatures who make me smile every day and subsequently inspired me to create this book.

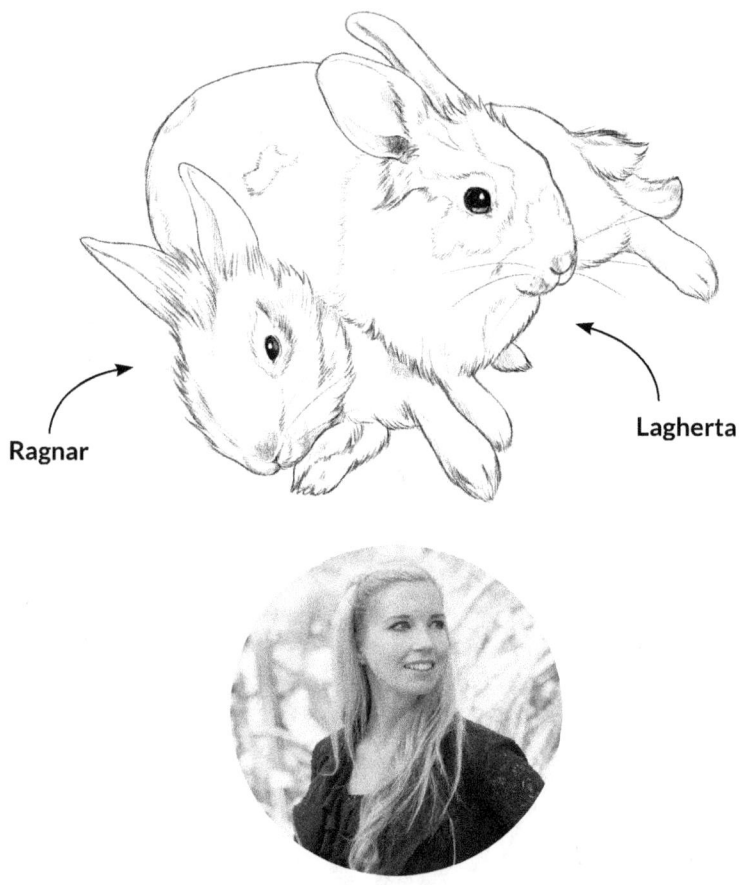

Lucille Solomon is an illustrator from Switzerland. She graduated from the Zurich University of the Arts with a bachelor's degree in Scientific Illustration. She now works as a designer and freelance scientific and medical illustrator. In her free time, she's always working on personal creative projects. She loves to create illustrations of cute animals, children's illustrations, and instructional online courses.

www.ingramcontent.com/pod-product-compliance
Lightning Source LLC
Chambersburg PA
CBHW050232230526
45470CB00005B/1917